HOW TO BUY A CAR AT THE DEALERSHIP

And Not Get Ripped Off That Bad

2ND EDITION

BENJAMIN A. TEMPLAR

SUNBOWMEDIA

ISBN: 978-1-968216-18-4

Ebook ISBN: 978-1-968216-19-1

Book Cover by Benjamin A. Templar

CONTENTS

INTRODUCTION

This book isn't about how to win at the dealership.

That's a fantasy.

This book is about how to **lose less**—because you will lose something. The trick is making sure it's not your **ass**.

Because, yes... you are going to get ripped off at the dealership.

And that sentence alone might bother some people. It might sound harsh. It might sound cynical. But it's not meant to discourage you.

☞ It's meant to prepare you.

A dealership is a business. A large one. With employees, buildings, inventory, overhead, and pressure to perform every single month.

They are not there to "give you a great deal."

They are there to:

☞ **make money on you**

And they are very good at it.

So the real question is not:

"Am I going to get ripped off?"

The real question is:

"How bad is it going to be?"

That's the entire purpose of this book.

Not perfection.

Not fantasy.

👉 **Minimization. Control. Awareness.**

A Reality Check Before We Begin

If you expect to walk into a dealership and outsmart every person in the building...

👉 This is not that book.

If you think you're going to completely avoid every dollar of profit...

👉 That's not realistic either.

And if you believe the dealership is going to sit across from you and say:

"Let's make sure you get the best possible deal at our expense."

👉 That will not happen.

What *will* happen is this:

They will guide the conversation
They will control the structure
They will present numbers in a way that benefits them
They will rely on your fatigue, your emotions, and your lack of information

And if you're not prepared...

You will agree to things you don't fully understand

What This Book Actually Gives You

This book gives you something much more valuable than "winning."

It gives you **clarity**

You will understand:

- How pricing is structured
- Where hidden profit lives
- Why monthly payments are used against you
- How financing is manipulated
- What fees are real—and which ones are not
- When to push
- When to pause
- And when to walk away

Because once you understand those things...

You stop being easy to work

And that changes everything.

Who This Book Is For (Important)

Let's be very clear about this:

This book is primarily written for buying a brand-new car at a dealership.

That is the main focus.

Now, will some of these strategies apply to used cars?

👉 Yes.

In fact, many of them will.

But the used car market is a different world:

Different pricing structures
Different risk levels
Different inspection concerns
Different negotiation dynamics

So while you will gain value if you're buying used...

👉 This book is built specifically for **new car dealership transactions**, with or without a trade-in.

That distinction matters.

Why This Second Edition Exists

The first version of this book was published in **2008**.

It was short. Direct. Basic.

Less than 50 pages.

At the time, it reflected what I knew then.

But that was nearly two decades ago.

Since then, I've had:

👉 Almost 20 years of additional experience

Buying.
Selling.
Leasing.
Negotiating.
Making mistakes.
Paying for those mistakes.

Sometimes with money.

Sometimes with frustration.

Sometimes with both.

The Expensive Education

Over the years, I've lost thousands of dollars.

Not because I wasn't intelligent.

Not because I didn't care.

But because I didn't understand:

👉 how the system actually works

I trusted numbers that were presented to me.
I focused on the wrong things.
I accepted fees I didn't question.
I negotiated in the wrong order.

And every one of those mistakes...

👉 had a price

What Changed

Eventually, something shifts.

You stop reacting.

You start seeing patterns.

You begin to recognize:

When numbers are being moved
When pressure is being applied
When "good deals" aren't actually good
When it's time to stop talking

And over time...

☞ You get better

Not perfect.

But better.

Where I Am Now

Today, I can confidently say this:

☞ Most of the time, I get very strong deals.

Not because I'm lucky.

Not because I'm aggressive.

But because I understand the structure.

And more importantly...

☞ I know when to walk away

My wife and I have saved thousands of dollars over the years by simply:

asking the right questions
ignoring the wrong ones
and refusing to move forward when something doesn't make sense

That's the difference.

What You Should Expect From This Book

This is not a theory book.

This is not a motivational book.

This is not a "feel good" guide.

This is a **practical, real-world playbook**.

You will see:

Real tactics
Real strategies
Real examples
Real language you can use

And most importantly:

👉 A way to think differently during the process

The Mindset Shift

Most people walk into a dealership thinking:

"I hope I get a good deal."

That mindset is passive.

This book shifts that to:

"I understand how this works—and I'm in control of my decisions."

That's a completely different position.

Final Thought Before You Begin

You don't need to memorize everything in this book.

You don't need to become an expert overnight.

But if you take just a few core ideas and apply them...

- you will spend less money
- you will feel more confident
- and you will avoid the most common traps

One Truth to Carry With You

You are not trying to beat the dealership.

- You are trying to avoid beating yourself.

Now let's begin.

🔥 PART I – UNDERSTAND THE GAME

You're Already Inside the System

⛔ WARNING ❗

"If you don't understand a term, jump to the Glossary at the end. It might be the most important section in this entire book."

Chapter 1

THE DEALERSHIP GAME 🎮

🍽️ You Are Their Lunch 🍱

Once upon a time, in wonderland...

You walk into a car dealership.

The lights are bright.
The floors are spotless.
The cars shine like they were just born.

Someone greets you with a smile.

"Hey! Welcome in. What brings you here today?"

Friendly. Relaxed. No pressure.

At least... that's how it feels.

But this isn't wonderland.

This is a game.

And the moment you step onto that lot...

👉 **You're already playing.**

The problem?

👉 Most people don't even know there's a game.

THE ILLUSION

To the average buyer, a dealership feels like:

A place to look at cars
A place to ask questions
A place to "figure things out"
A place where someone helps you buy something

That's the illusion.

Because underneath that surface...

👉 It's not a store.

👉 It's a **structured sales environment designed to extract maximum profit per customer.**

That doesn't make it evil.

But it does make it **intentional**.

IN DEFENSE OF THE DEALERSHIP

Let's be clear about something.

This is not a "hate the dealership" book.

Dealerships are businesses.

They have:

Payroll
Inventory costs
Financing expenses

Marketing budgets
Pressure to perform

And most importantly...

👉 **They exist to make money.**

Not to give deals.
Not to educate buyers.
Not to "hook you up."

Those things can happen...

...but only when they align with profit.

THE REAL JOB OF A SALESPERSON

You might think the salesperson's job is:

👉 "To help you find the right car."

That's what it looks like.

That's what it feels like.

That's what they say.

But their real job is:

👉 **To move you from interest... to commitment... to signature.**

As efficiently as possible.

With the highest profit possible.

Without you walking away.

They Are Trained

This part matters more than anything.

👉 **Car salespeople are not winging it.**

They are trained.

Not casually.

Not occasionally.

👉 **Systematically.**

They are trained on:

How to build rapport quickly
How to ask questions that guide you
How to control the conversation
How to redirect objections
How to frame numbers
How to present payments instead of prices
How to keep you emotionally engaged

And most importantly...

👉 **How to close.**

You... Are Not

Here's the imbalance.

They do this:

👉 Every day
👉 All day

☞ With hundreds... sometimes thousands... of customers

You?

☞ You do this once every few years.

Maybe.

So when you walk in...

It's not:

☞ Buyer vs. Seller

It's:

☞ **Amateur vs. Professional**

THE GAME IS NOT ABOUT CARS

This is where most people get it wrong.

They think the game is about:

Horsepower
Features
Colors
Trim levels

It's not.

☞ The car is the **object**.

The real game is about:

☞ **Money structure**

Price
Payment
Interest rate
Trade-in
Add-ons
Terms

And how those numbers are presented, moved, hidden, or combined.

THE BATTLEFIELD

Once you understand that...

You start to see the dealership differently.

It's not random.

It's designed.

There are stages:

The Greeting
The Needs Assessment
The Vehicle Selection
The Test Drive
The Desk (Negotiation)
The Finance Office (F&I)

Each stage has a purpose.

Each stage has strategies.

Each stage moves you closer to one thing:

👉 **Signing.**

THE MOST IMPORTANT QUESTION

There is one question that silently controls everything:

👉 **Who gets tired first?**

Because this game is not just about logic.

It's about:

Time
Pressure
Emotion
Fatigue

You came in excited.

But after:

2 hours
3 hours
Maybe 4 hours

Your brain changes.

You get tired.

You want it to be over.

And that's when this happens:

👉 "You know what... fine. Let's just do it."

THE PATIENCE ADVANTAGE

Here's the truth most people never realize:

👉 **The dealership can outlast you.**

They are:

In their environment
On their schedule
In control of the process

They can:

Leave the room
"Talk to the manager"
Reset the conversation
Bring new numbers
Keep you waiting

And every minute that passes...

👉 Your resistance drops.

EMOTIONAL ENGINEERING

This isn't accidental.

It's designed.

You'll feel:

Excitement
Urgency
Relief

Confusion
Pressure

All in the same visit.

One moment:

👉 "This is a great deal."

Next moment:

👉 "Wait... what just happened?"

That emotional fluctuation is not random.

👉 It's part of the process.

THE FRIENDLY TRAP

Here's one of the most powerful elements.

The salesperson is:

Friendly
Relatable
Likeable

They might:

Joke with you
Agree with you
"Fight for you" with the manager

You start to feel:

👉 "This person is on my side."

But remember this:

👉 **They are on the dealership's side.**

Always.

Even if they like you.

Even if they're honest.

Even if they're a good person.

THIS IS NOT PERSONAL

This is important.

Most buyers think:

👉 "If I'm nice, they'll treat me better."

That's not how it works.

This isn't about:

You being liked
You being respected
You being smart

This is about:

👉 **The structure of the deal.**

THE MOMENT EVERYTHING CHANGES

Once you understand this...

Everything shifts.

You stop saying:

👉 "They're helping me buy a car."

And you start saying:

👉 **"I'm inside a system designed to sell me a car."**

That's a completely different mindset.

THE NEW FRAME

From this point forward, you are not:

A shopper
A visitor
A "potential buyer"

👉 You are a **player in the game.**

And the goal is simple:

👉 **Don't play their game blindly.**

Key Principle

The dealership is not trying to cheat you.

👉 They are trying to **win.**

And if you don't understand the rules...

☞ You become the easiest way for them to do it.

Bottom Line

The moment you step into a dealership...

☞ The game begins.

You don't have to be aggressive.

You don't have to be confrontational.

But you do need to be:

☞ **Aware**

Because once you see the game...

☞ You stop being the target.

And you start becoming:

☞ **The one in control.**

Chapter 2

DO YOUR HOMEWORK!

The Work You Do Before the Deal Is the Deal: Preparation Wins the Deal

> "You have to do your (home) work. It's an incumbent upon use as the buyer to do the work. If you don't, you will end up being taking advantage of."
>
> — RAY SHEFSKA

Most people think the deal starts at the dealership.

It doesn't.

The deal starts **before you ever leave your house.**

And here's the truth that most buyers never hear:

The person who is more prepared... wins.

Not the smartest.
Not the most confident.
Not the most aggressive.

The most prepared.

WHY PREPARATION MATTERS MORE THAN NEGOTIATION

You can be:

Confident
Calm
Polite
Even experienced

And still lose thousands of dollars.

Why?

Because without preparation:

👉 You are guessing.

You're reacting to:

numbers you've never seen
terms you don't fully understand
structures you didn't plan for

And the moment you start reacting...

👉 You lose control.

THE DEALERSHIP'S ADVANTAGE

Let's be clear:

They already did their homework.

They know:

The car's true cost
The incentives available
Your likely credit range
Market pricing
How to structure the deal

You?

If you walk in unprepared...

👉 You're walking into their system blind.

YOUR ADVANTAGE (IF YOU USE IT)

You don't need to know everything.

But you do need to know enough to:

👉 **Recognize what's real... and what's not.**

That comes from preparation.

Step 1 – Know the Car Before You See the Car

Never walk into a dealership "just to look."

That's how you get pulled into the process too early.

Before you go:

👉 Decide exactly what you want.

Make and model
Trim level
Key features
Must-haves vs. nice-to-haves

Because if you don't decide...

👉 The salesperson will decide for you.

Step 2 – Understand Market Pricing

This is where most buyers fail.

They rely on:

MSRP
The dealership
The salesperson

Instead of the market.

Your job is to answer one question:

👉 *What is this car actually selling for right now?*

Not:

what it's listed for
not what they say
not what it "should be"

👉 What it is **actually selling for**

How You Do That

Check multiple sources:

Dealership websites
Online listings
National pricing tools
Inventory across multiple dealers

Look at:

Same trim
Same configuration
Similar location

After reviewing 4–5 dealerships...

👉 You will start seeing patterns.

That pattern is:

👉 **The real price range**

Step 3 – Know Your Trade-In Value (Before They Do)

If you're trading in a car:

👉 You must know its value before they tell you.

Use:

Kelley Blue Book (KBB)
Carvana
Other online appraisal tools

Enter:

VIN
Mileage
Condition

Get at least 2–3 estimates.

This gives you:

👉 A realistic range

Now when they offer you a number...

👉 You don't guess.

👉 You compare.

Step 4 – Secure Your Financing (Or At Least Your Baseline)

This is one of the biggest advantages you can have.

Before going to the dealership:

👉 Get pre-approved.

From:

A credit union
Your bank
A trusted lender

This gives you:

A real interest rate
A real loan structure
A baseline

Now when the dealership offers financing:

👉 You're not blind.

You're comparing.

Step 5 – Know Your Numbers

Before you walk in, you should already know:

Your maximum budget
Your ideal monthly payment
Your down payment range
Your walk-away number

Not vague.

👉 Defined.

Because if you don't define your limits...

👉 The dealership will define them for you.

Step 6 – Bring the Right Tools

Preparation is not just knowledge.

It's execution.

Bring:

A calculator (or phone ready)
Notes or saved pricing
Trade-in estimates
Financing pre-approval

Why?

Because when numbers start moving...

👉 You need to move with them.

Step 7 – Prepare for Time (This Matters More Than You Think)

The dealership experience is designed to take time.

Hours.

Not minutes.

That's intentional.

Because time creates:

fatigue
impatience
emotional decisions

So prepare for it.

👉 Eat before you go
👉 Bring water
👉 Don't schedule anything after

Because once you feel rushed...

👉 You become easier to close.

The Endurance Factor

Most people don't lose because they're tricked.

They lose because they get tired.

They say:

👉 "Let's just finish this."

That sentence...

👉 is where money disappears.

Step 8 – Use the Internet (Your Biggest Weapon)

This is the modern advantage buyers have.

Dealerships used to control information.

Now you do.

You can:

Compare pricing instantly
Check inventory
Verify claims
Research incentives
Contact multiple dealers

And here's the key:

👉 You don't have to step into a dealership to start negotiating.

You can begin:

👉 By email
👉 By phone
👉 By collecting OTD estimates

This changes everything.

The Shift

When you prepare properly...

Something powerful happens.

You stop being:

👉 A customer looking for help

And you become:

👉 A buyer with options

And options create:

👉 Leverage

What Preparation Really Does

Preparation doesn't guarantee a perfect deal.

But it does guarantee this:

👉 You won't be easy.

And in a system designed to profit from unprepared buyers...

👉 That alone changes the outcome.

Key Principle

You don't win at the dealership by reacting.

👉 You win by arriving ready.

. . .

Bottom Line

The dealership is where the deal is finalized.

👉 Not where it is decided.

The real deal...

👉 Is built before you walk in.

And if you do the work...

👉 You don't just participate in the process.

You control it.

Chapter 3

CREDIT, LEVERAGE & CONTROL

Handcuffed for the Life of the Loan

Most buyers think of credit as one thing:

👉 "Will I get approved or not?"

That's it.

A yes or no.

But inside a dealership...

👉 Your credit is not just approval.

👉 **It's leverage.**

And how that leverage is used—by you or by them—can change the entire deal.

WHAT YOUR CREDIT REALLY REPRESENTS

Your credit score is more than a number.

It represents:

Risk
Predictability
Borrowing behavior
Financial discipline

To a lender, it answers one question:

☞ *How likely are you to pay this money back?*

But to a dealership?

☞ It answers a different question:

☞ *How much room do we have to work this deal?*

THE CREDIT SPECTRUM

In simple terms, buyers fall into categories:

Excellent Credit (720+)
Good Credit (660–719)
Fair Credit (600–659)
Subprime (below 600)

Each category affects:

Interest rate
Loan approval
Deal structure
Negotiation power

But here's the key:

☞ The dealership sees these categories not as labels...

☞ But as opportunities.

WHY THEY WANT YOUR CREDIT EARLY

One of the first things you'll hear is:

"Let's run your credit real quick."

Or:

"We just need to see what you qualify for."

Sounds harmless.

Even helpful.

But timing matters.

👉 **When they pull your credit early... they gain control early.**

WHAT HAPPENS BEHIND THE SCENES

Once your credit is pulled:

Your score is known
Your risk level is known
Your financing options are known

But most importantly:

👉 **Your negotiating position becomes visible to them.**

Now they know:

How flexible you can be
What rate you might accept
How much they can structure into the deal

And you?

👉 You still don't know anything yet.

THE INFORMATION IMBALANCE

This is where the game tilts.

They know:

Your credit tier
Your likely approval range
Your financing options

You don't know:

The buy rate
The lender terms
The markup potential

👉 That imbalance is leverage.

And if you give it up too early...

👉 You're negotiating from behind.

CREDIT AS A TOOL (NOT A WEAKNESS)

Most people feel vulnerable about their credit.

They think:

"What if it's not good enough?"
"What if I don't get approved?"

So they rush to find out.

But here's the shift:

👉 Your credit is not something to reveal early.

👉 It's something to **use strategically.**

THE POWER OF PRE-APPROVAL

This is where everything changes.

Before you walk into a dealership:

👉 Get pre-approved.

From:

A credit union
Your bank
A trusted lender

Now you walk in knowing:

Your interest rate
Your loan terms
Your approval status

WHAT THIS DOES

It flips the dynamic.

Instead of asking:

👉 "Can I get approved?"

You're saying:

👉 "I already am."

Now the dealership must:

Match it
Beat it
Or lose the deal

That's leverage.

THE INTEREST RATE GAME

Here's something most buyers never realize:

☞ The rate you're offered is not always the rate you earned.

There are two rates:

Buy Rate — what the bank approves
Sell Rate — what the dealer offers you

The difference?

☞ Profit.

And if you don't know your baseline...

☞ You won't even see it.

CREDIT AFFECTS MORE THAN THE RATE

Your credit doesn't just influence interest.

It influences:

Loan length
Down payment expectations

Monthly payment structure
Add-on positioning
Negotiation flexibility

In other words:

👉 It shapes the entire deal.

THE "PAYMENT FOCUS" TRAP

When they know your credit early...

They can do this:

👉 Structure the deal around a payment

Instead of showing:

Price
Rate
Total cost

They show:

👉 "This works for your budget."

And suddenly:

👉 You're not negotiating a deal anymore.

👉 You're accepting a payment.

WHEN SHOULD YOU SHARE YOUR CREDIT?

Not at the beginning.

Not during the early conversation.

👉 Only when:

You've established pricing
You understand the structure
You're ready to finalize

Because until then...

👉 It gives them more than it gives you.

THE CONFIDENCE SHIFT

When you understand your credit...

You walk differently.

You speak differently.

You negotiate differently.

Because you're not hoping.

👉 You're deciding.

THE SILENT TRUTH

Dealerships don't fear buyers with bad credit.

They expect them.

They work around them.

They structure deals for them.

But what they respect?

👉 Buyers who understand their credit.

Key Principle

Your credit is not just about approval.

👉 It's about control.

Bottom Line

If you don't know your credit...

👉 They will use it against you.

If you reveal it too early...

👉 You give up leverage.

But if you understand it, prepare it, and use it correctly...

👉 It becomes one of your strongest advantages in the entire deal.

THE NEGATIVE EQUITY TRAP: THE DEBT THAT FOLLOWS YOU

There is something happening in the car market right now...

...and most buyers have no idea how dangerous it is.

It's called **negative equity**.

And it is quietly trapping millions of people in a cycle they can't escape.

What "Negative Equity" Really Means

Negative equity simply means:

👉 You owe more on your car than the car is worth.

You are "underwater."

And today...

👉 This is not rare.
👉 This is becoming normal.

Recent data shows that:

30.9% of all trade-ins have negative equity
The **average amount owed above value: $7,183**

That's not a small gap.

That's a financial anchor.

The Problem Isn't Just the Debt—It's the Timing

Here's what most people don't realize:

When you finance a car...

👉 You are almost always losing money at the beginning of the loan.

The car depreciates fast.

Your loan balance decreases slowly.

Which means:

👉 For years... you are upside down.

In today's market, with longer loans...

👉 You may not reach break-even until **5–6 years into the loan**.

And yet...

Most people try to trade in their car around:

👉 **3–4 years.**

That's where everything breaks.

The Math No One Explains to You

Let's look at what's actually happening:

Average loan terms are now **72 to 84 months (6–7 years)**
The average loan for buyers with negative equity: **77.4 months**
Nearly **90% of these loans are 72 months or longer**

43% are 84 months or longer

Now combine that with:

Rising car prices (near $50,000+)
Higher interest rates (around **7.9% or more**)

And you get this:

👉 You're financing more
👉 For longer
👉 At a higher rate

That's not one problem.

👉 That's a **triple trap**.

How the Trap Gets Worse

Let's say you owe:

👉 $30,000 on your current car
But it's only worth:
👉 $23,000

You're **$7,000 underwater**.

Now you go to a dealership.

They say:

"Don't worry—we'll take care of that."

What they actually do:

👉 They add that $7,000 to your next loan.

Now your new loan isn't just for the new car.

👉 It includes your old debt.

And just like that...

👉 The cycle continues.

The Real Cost of Rolling Debt Forward

When you roll negative equity into a new loan:

You finance **more than the car is worth**
Your monthly payment goes up
Your loan term gets extended
You build equity even slower

In real numbers:

Average financed amount: **~$56,000**
Average monthly payment: **$932/month**
Total interest paid: **~$15,000+**

Compare that to a typical buyer:

👉 Less than $10,000 in interest

That's a massive difference.

And Here's the Hard Truth

The dealership...

👉 Does not carry this risk.

The salesperson...

☞ Does not carry this risk.

The bank...

☞ Minimizes their risk through terms and structure.

☞ **You carry the risk.**

It is your debt.

It is your obligation.

And once you sign:

☞ It's yours for **72–84 months.**

No one will care about it more than you.

Why This Is Becoming a Crisis

This isn't just individual behavior anymore.

It's structural.

We're now seeing:

Record levels of **loan delinquencies**
Nearly **2 million vehicle repossessions in a year**
Rising used car prices
New car prices approaching **$50,000+**

At the same time:

☞ People are holding onto cars longer

👉 But still can't reach positive equity

That's a broken system.

What This Means for You

You need to understand one thing:

👉 A car is not an appreciating asset.

It will lose value.

Every time.

So your strategy must change.

How to Avoid the Trap

✅ 1. KNOW YOUR NUMBERS

Call your lender.

Find out:

👉 Your exact payoff amount

Then find out what your car is actually worth in the market.

Not guesses.

👉 Real offers.

✅ 2. DO NOT ROLL NEGATIVE EQUITY FORWARD

This is the biggest mistake.

👉 It feels easy now...
👉 It costs you later.

Sometimes the smartest move is:

👉 **Do nothing.**
👉 Keep the car longer.

✅ 3. STOP BUYING THE PAYMENT

Monthly payments can be manipulated.

👉 Focus on the **total price** and the **total loan**.

Always.

✅ 4. IF YOU'RE STRUGGLING—CALL YOUR LENDER

Before you miss payments.

Before things get worse.

Most lenders:

👉 Do NOT want your car.

They want the loan to perform.

And they may:

Adjust terms

Offer temporary relief
Help you avoid repossession

THE REALITY NO ONE TELLS YOU

Sometimes...

👉 The best financial move is not upgrading.

It's staying where you are.

Driving your current car longer.

Letting the loan catch up.

Building equity the slow way.

Final Thought

The dealership will always offer you a way out.

But not always a better one.

Because their goal is:

👉 To move cars.

Your goal must be:

👉 To protect your financial future.

THE CREDIT LOCK STRATEGY: SHUT THE DOOR BEFORE THEY OPEN IT

A friend of mine, Javier, shared a simple strategy with me...

...and it might be one of the most underrated ways to protect yourself inside a dealership.

👉 **Lock your credit before you walk in.**

Not after.
Not "if something feels off."
👉 **Before.**

Why This Matters

When a dealership runs your credit, they can:

Send your application to multiple lenders
Generate multiple credit inquiries
Start structuring deals without your full control

Sometimes even faster than you expect.

And once that happens...

👉 You are reacting to the deal
instead of controlling it.

The Hidden Risk

Many buyers assume:

"I'll just give permission when I'm ready."

But in reality:

You may be asked for your driver's license early
Your information may already be in the system
The process may start before you clearly approve it

And even if everything is "technically allowed"...

☞ It doesn't mean it's in your best interest.

What a Credit Lock Actually Does

A credit lock (or freeze) blocks access to your credit report.

That means:

☞ No lender
☞ No dealership
☞ No third party

...can run your credit without your approval.

Even if they try.

☞ **It simply won't go through.**

The Three Major Credit Bureaus

To fully protect yourself, you need to lock your credit with all three:

1. EXPERIAN

☞ www.experian.com

Create a free account

Go to "Credit Lock" or "Security Freeze"
Enable the lock

✓ You can unlock it instantly from your phone
✓ You can set temporary access windows

2. EQUIFAX

☞ www.equifax.com

Create a free account
Navigate to "Credit Freeze"
Activate the freeze

✓ You can schedule a temporary lift
✓ You can remove it for a specific timeframe

3. TRANSUNION

☞ www.transunion.com

Create an account
Go to "Credit Freeze" section
Turn it on

✓ Allows temporary unlocks
✓ Can be managed in real time

Important Note About Carfax

Carfax is **not** a credit bureau.

☞ It provides vehicle history reports, not credit checks.

So locking your credit there won't do anything.

👉 The protection happens through:

Experian
Equifax
TransUnion

How to Use This Strategy at the Dealership

This is where it becomes powerful.

STEP 1 – WALK IN WITH YOUR CREDIT LOCKED

Now:

👉 No one can run your credit without you knowing

STEP 2 – CONTROL THE TIMING

When you're **ready** to move forward:

Log into your accounts
Unlock your credit temporarily
Allow access for a short window (e.g., 24–48 hours)

Then:

👉 Lock it again

STEP 3 – CONTROL HOW MANY LENDERS SEE YOUR CREDIT

You can now ask:

👉 "How many lenders are you submitting my application to?"

If they say:

"10... 15... 20..."

You respond:

👉 "No. Limit it to 3–5."

Why This Matters More Than You Think

Each credit check can:

Affect your credit profile
Create unnecessary inquiries
Open the door to rate manipulation

Yes—auto loan inquiries within a short window are often grouped for scoring purposes...

👉 But that doesn't mean unlimited checks are harmless.

More lenders = more variables = less control.

What This Strategy Really Does

This isn't just about protecting your credit.

👉 It's about controlling the process.

Instead of:

Dealership → runs your credit → builds the deal → presents it to you

You flip it to:

☞ You → authorize access → define limits → control the timing

Final Thought

Most buyers try to control the deal **after it starts**.

That's already too late.

This strategy does something different:

☞ It prevents the deal from starting without you.

And that changes everything.

⚔ PART II – HOW THEY CONTROL YOU

You Think You're Choosing. You're Not.

Chapter 4

HOW THEY CONTROL THE DEAL

How They Steer You without You Realizing It

You walk into a dealership thinking one thing:

👉 *"I'm here to choose a car."*

That's what it feels like.

That's what it looks like.

But in reality...

👉 **You are being guided.**

Not forced.
Not pressured (at least not yet).
Not manipulated in an obvious way.

👉 Guided.

And the most effective control...

👉 is the kind you don't notice.

THE FIRST SHIFT

It starts early.

Very early.

You might say:

"I'm looking for a truck."

And the response comes:

"Great. Let me show you something."

Not:

"Let me show you *all* your options."

👉 Just... something.

One vehicle.
One direction.
One path.

And once that happens...

👉 The field narrows.

THEY DON'T SHOW YOU CARS

They Show You **Paths**

You think you're exploring.

But what you're really doing is:

👉 Moving through a **pre-selected path**

They don't need to show you everything.

They only need to show you:

👉 What moves the deal forward.

That could be:

What they have too much of
What has the highest profit
What fits your "payment range"
What is easiest to close

THE CAR SELECTION ILLUSION

Here's the subtle trick:

They don't say:

👉 "You should buy this car."

They say:

👉 "Let's take a look at this one."

And once you look...

👉 You start imagining.

"This feels nice."
"I could see myself in this."
"This might work..."

And now the shift happens:

👉 You're no longer choosing a category.

👉 You're emotionally attached to a specific vehicle.

THE TEST DRIVE TRAP

The test drive feels harmless.

Fun, even.

But it serves one purpose:

👉 **Attachment**

Once you drive the car:

You feel it
You hear it
You imagine owning it

And suddenly:

👉 It's not "a car" anymore.

👉 It's *your car*.

That emotional shift changes everything.

Because now the conversation becomes:

👉 "How do we make this work?"

Instead of:

👉 "Is this the right deal?"

THE MONTHLY PAYMENT PIVOT

This is where control becomes invisible.

At some point, you'll hear:

"What kind of monthly payment are you looking for?"

That question sounds normal.

Helpful.

Even necessary.

But it's one of the most important shifts in the entire process.

Because the moment you answer...

☞ The deal stops being about price.

☞ And starts being about **payment.**

Why This Matters

When you focus on price:

☞ Everything is visible.

When you focus on payment:

☞ Everything can be hidden.

They can:

Extend the loan term
Adjust the interest rate
Move numbers between categories
Add products quietly

And still land on a number that "works."

THE CONTROL EQUATION

Here's what they're managing behind the scenes:

Vehicle price
Trade-in value
Down payment
Interest rate
Loan term
Add-ons

That's six moving pieces.

You?

👉 You're looking at one number.

👉 Monthly payment.

That's not a negotiation.

👉 That's a **controlled outcome.**

THE "GOOD NEWS" TECHNIQUE

You'll hear something like:

"Good news—we got you where you wanted to be."

And they show you:

👉 A payment.

Not the breakdown.
Not the structure.
Not the full picture.

Just the result.

And if that number feels comfortable...

👉 Most people accept it.

THE MANAGER DISAPPEARANCE ACT

Another control tactic:

The salesperson leaves the room.

"Let me talk to my manager."

Now you're waiting.

Time passes.

Energy drops.

And when they return...

👉 They bring a new number.

This does two things:

It creates the illusion of effort
It resets your expectations

Now you're reacting again.

THE GUIDED YES

At no point do they say:

👉 "You have to do this."

Instead, they guide you toward saying:

👉 "Yes."

Yes to the car
Yes to the payment
Yes to the structure
Yes to the deal

And each "yes" makes the next one easier.

THE SUBTLE CONTROL

This is what makes the system powerful.

It doesn't feel aggressive.

It feels:

Helpful
Logical
Smooth

And that's why it works.

Because you don't resist what you don't recognize.

THE MOMENT OF REALIZATION

At the end, many buyers feel something strange.

Not regret.

Not confusion.

Just a quiet thought:

👉 "I think I did okay..."

But they don't really know.

Because they never saw the full picture.

BREAKING THE CONTROL

Once you understand this...

You start doing things differently.

You:

Decide the car before you go
Focus on total price, not payment
Control the timing of the deal
Ask for full breakdowns
Refuse to move forward without clarity

And suddenly:

👉 The process slows down.

👉 The control shifts.

. . .

Key Principle

They don't control the deal by force.

👉 They control it by **guiding your decisions.**

Bottom Line

You are not being pushed.

👉 You are being steered.

And if you don't recognize the steering...

👉 You end up exactly where they want you.

But once you see it...

👉 You don't just follow the path.

👉 You choose it.

Chapter 5

THE HIDDEN PSYCHOLOGY TRICKS

Psychokinesising Your Dollars 🧠💸

👉 *"The biggest risk isn't the dealership... it's **you**."*

Not in a blaming way—
in an **awareness way**.

This is the chapter that makes everything else in the book *stick*.

HOW THE DEAL GETS DECIDED IN YOUR MIND BEFORE IT GETS SIGNED ON PAPER

Most people think they lose money at the dealership because of numbers.

Price
Interest rate
Fees

That's what it looks like.

But the truth is:

👉 **The deal is decided long before the numbers show up.**

It's decided in your head.

THE REAL BATTLEFIELD

You don't lose the deal on paper.

👉 You lose it internally.

When something *feels* right
When something *sounds* reasonable
When something *looks* like a good deal

That's where decisions are made.

And once the decision is made...

👉 The numbers simply justify it.

THE SHIRT EFFECT

Imagine you walk into a dealership wearing:

A sharp shirt
Clean shoes
Put-together appearance

Versus walking in:

Rushed
Casual
Disorganized

Do you think you get treated the same?

👉 You don't.

This isn't about respect.

It's about perception.

And perception affects:

How they approach you
How seriously they take you
How they structure the deal

But here's the deeper layer:

👉 It also affects **you.**

When you feel confident...

You think clearly.

When you feel unsure...

👉 You become easier to guide.

THE FUNNEL YOU NEVER SEE (THE "95421" EFFECT)

There's a pattern most buyers go through.

Not intentionally.

But consistently.

You walk in thinking:

👉 "I'm just browsing."

Then it becomes:

👉 "I'm narrowing it down."

Then:

👉 "This one looks good."

Then:

👉 "I could see myself in this."

Then:

👉 "Let's see if we can make it work."

And finally:

👉 "Let's just do it."

That's the funnel.

Not forced.

👉 **Progressive commitment.**

Each step feels small.

But each step removes your ability to walk away.

THE CAR DOESN'T CHOOSE YOU... UNTIL IT DOES

At the beginning, you're evaluating cars.

Logical. Detached.

But something happens during the process:

You sit in the car
You adjust the seat

You touch the wheel
You test the sound system

And without realizing it...

👉 You start picturing your life with it.

Now the shift happens:

👉 It's no longer *a car.*

👉 It's *your car.*

EMOTIONAL ATTACHMENT CHANGES EVERYTHING

Once that happens:

You stop comparing
You stop questioning
You stop exploring alternatives

Now your brain is doing something different:

👉 It's trying to **justify keeping it.**

That's when thoughts like this appear:

"It's only a little more..."
"I deserve it..."
"This feels right..."

And at that point:

👉 Logic is no longer in control.

THE COMFORT TRAP

Dealerships are designed to make you comfortable.

Climate-controlled environment
Friendly conversation
Relaxed seating
Casual tone

Why?

Because comfort lowers resistance.

When you're comfortable:

👉 You don't feel like you're in a negotiation.

You feel like:

👉 You're making a decision.

THE TIME EFFECT (AGAIN, BUT DEEPER)

Time doesn't just make you tired.

👉 It makes you **commit.**

The longer you stay:

The more time you've invested
The more effort you've given
The more "real" the deal feels

And your brain starts thinking:

👉 "I've already come this far..."

That's called:

👉 **Sunk cost thinking**

And it's one of the strongest psychological traps there is.

THE FEAR OF LOSING THE CAR

At some point, you may hear:

"This one might not be here tomorrow."

Sometimes it's true.

Sometimes it's not.

But the effect is the same:

👉 You feel pressure.

And pressure creates urgency.

And urgency kills analysis.

THE NEED TO "WIN"

Here's another subtle one.

You don't just want a car.

👉 You want to feel like you got a good deal.

So when they say:

"We worked really hard to get you here..."

You feel like:

☞ You won.

Even if the numbers say otherwise.

THE IDENTITY SHIFT

At the beginning, you're a shopper.

At the end, you feel like:

☞ An owner.

And once you feel like an owner...

☞ Walking away becomes emotionally difficult.

Because now you're not giving up a car.

☞ You're giving up *your car*.

THE SILENT AGREEMENT

There's a moment in every deal where you stop questioning.

You don't say it out loud.

But internally, you decide:

☞ "I'm probably going to do this."

And once that happens...

👉 Everything after that is just execution.

THE ONLY WAY TO BREAK IT

You don't beat psychology by being smarter.

👉 You beat it by being aware.

By recognizing:

When you're getting attached
When you're feeling pressure
When you're justifying instead of analyzing

And asking one question:

👉 "Would I make this same decision if I walked away and came back tomorrow?"

Key Principle

You don't lose the deal because of numbers.

👉 You lose it because of how you feel about them.

Bottom Line

The dealership doesn't need to trick you.

👉 Your mind does most of the work.

All they have to do...

👉 Is guide it in the right direction.

But once you see the patterns...

👉 You stop reacting emotionally.

And you start deciding:

👉 Intentionally.

THE TEST DRIVE SCAM 🚗

One of the first moves the dealership makes is not about price.

It's not about the car.

It's not even about your needs.

It's about getting you physically inside the dealership as fast as possible.

Because the moment you are there...

👉 The game changes.

The Rush to Get You In

Have you noticed how fast they try to move you from:

Online →
Phone →
In person

It happens almost immediately.

You ask a simple question like:

"Do you have this car available?"
Or
"What's the price on this model?"

And instead of answering clearly, they respond with something like:

"When would you like to come in?"
"When can we schedule your test drive?"

"We have availability this afternoon or tomorrow morning."

They don't even ask **if** you want a test drive.

They ask **when**.

That's not an accident.

That's strategy.

Why They Want You There So Fast

Because the sooner they get you in...

👉 The less prepared you are.

👉 The more emotional you become.

👉 The easier it is for them to control the process.

Once you are physically there:

You've already invested time
You've already made an effort
You're less likely to walk away empty-handed

And most importantly:

👉 You are now inside their system.

The desk.
The waiting.
The "let me talk to my manager."
The back-and-forth.

That's where they make their money.

The Catnip: The Test Drive

The test drive is their catnip.

Cats can't resist catnip.

And most buyers...

👉 Can't resist a test drive.

They present it like a treat:

"Do you want to drive it?"
"Let's take it out for a spin."
"You're going to love it."

It feels exciting.

It feels harmless.

It feels like part of the process.

But the truth is:

👉 They don't care about you driving the car.

They care about you being there.

Because once you're there...

👉 You become their prey.

And they're ready to have you for lunch.

Brand New Car? You Don't Need a Test Drive

This might sound controversial, but it's true.

If you are buying a **brand new car**, you do not need a test drive.

Why?

Because:

You already know what the car is
You've seen reviews
You've done research
You know how it drives

A brand new car is not a mystery.

It's a product.

The test drive is not adding real value at that stage.

It's adding **emotional attachment**.

And emotional attachment is one of the strongest tools they have.

Because once you drive it...

Once you feel it...

Once you imagine it being yours...

👉 Your negotiation power drops.

Used Car? Different Story

Now, if you are buying a **used car**, that's different.

A test drive can absolutely make sense.

You want to:

Feel the car
Hear the engine
Check how it drives
Make sure nothing feels off

That is reasonable.

That is smart.

But here's the key:

👉 Not before securing the numbers.

The Right Way to Handle It

If it's a used car:

Get the **OTD price first (by email if possible)**
Get a **general trade-in idea if possible**

Then...

👉 Schedule the test drive.

Not the other way around.

Because if you go there first...

You are walking into the negotiation blind.

The Trade-In Excuse

Here's another classic line you will hear:

"We can't give you a trade-in value without seeing the car."

Sounds reasonable.

Sounds logical.

And sometimes, yes—it can be valid.

But here's the reality:

👉 In many cases, they don't even really inspect your car.

You bring your trade-in.

You expect a full inspection.

And what happens?

They look at it from a distance
Maybe walk around it once
Maybe not even that

And then they come back with a number.

That's it.

No deep inspection.
No serious evaluation.

So what does that tell you?

👉 In many cases, they already had a number in mind.

The "we need to see the car" line is often just a way to:

Get you physically there
Delay giving you numbers
Keep control of the conversation

What You Should Do Instead

Before stepping into any dealership, you should already:

Know the approximate **market value of your trade-in**
Have estimates from:
Carvana
Kelley Blue Book
Other platforms

So when they give you a number...

👉 You know if it's real or not.

THE DRIVER'S LICENSE TRAP-SCAM: WHEN THE DEAL STARTS WITHOUT YOU

One of the most harmless-looking moments in a dealership...

...is also one of the most dangerous.

It usually happens within the first few minutes.

"Can I grab your driver's license real quick?"
"It's just for the test drive."
"Insurance purposes."

Sounds reasonable.

Feels standard.

Most people hand it over without thinking.

And that's exactly the point.

The Moment You Hand It Over... Everything Changes

The second your driver's license is scanned or copied...

- You are no longer just a shopper.
- You become a profile.

Your:

Full legal name
Address
Date of birth

...are now inside their system.

And that's all they need to start building a strategy around you.

Not with you.

👉 Around you.

What They Can Do With That Information

While you think you're casually browsing...
or enjoying a test drive...

...the dealership may already be working behind the scenes.

They can:

Match you to internal customer records
Cross-reference databases
Identify prior buying behavior
Estimate your financial profile

And in some cases...

👉 Even initiate credit activity.

Yes—**even without your Social Security number.**

Under the Fair Credit Reporting Act (FCRA), what's required is not your SSN...

👉 It's something called *permissible purpose.*

Meaning:

If they claim a valid reason and have enough identifying information...

👉 A credit inquiry can still be triggered.

Most buyers have absolutely no idea this is possible.

Meanwhile... You're Just Driving the Car

You're thinking:

"This car feels great."
"This is smooth."
"I like this."

Of course it does.

👉 It's a brand-new car.

That test drive?

It's not about the car.

👉 It's about **you getting emotionally attached while they gather leverage.**

The Real Game Happening Behind the Scenes

While you're outside...

👉 The deal may already be taking shape.

They are estimating:

What monthly payment you'll accept
How much profit margin they can build in
Which lenders they can route you through
What add-ons they can successfully "pack" into your loan

They're not guessing.

👉 They're preparing.

By the time you sit down...

👉 They already have a plan for you.

How They Adjust Based on You

Once you're profiled, they adapt their strategy:

If you seem **payment-focused** → they push monthly payments
If you seem **price-focused** → they slow down and redirect
If you look like an **easy approval** → they expand the deal

You think the conversation is starting.

👉 It already started without you.

The Truth About the Test Drive

Let's be honest:

A brand-new car will almost always:

Drive smoothly
Feel comfortable
Impress you

So why the rush?

Why do they push the test drive so early?

Because:

👉 The faster you drive it...

👉 The faster you feel it...
👉 The faster you imagine owning it...

...and the faster your logic takes a back seat.

What You Should Do Instead

You don't need to be aggressive.

You just need to be intentional.

✅ **Control your information**

You can say:

"I'm happy to show my license, but I'm not authorizing any data use or credit activity."

✅ **Delay the test drive**

There is no rule that says you must drive the car immediately.

You can:

Review numbers first
Discuss pricing first
Stay in control first

✅ **Don't let the deal start without you**

Because once they begin building the deal...

👉 You are reacting.
👉 Not negotiating.

The Simple Truth

The dealership does **not** need your personal data to let you drive a car.

But they **want it badly**.

Because it gives them something incredibly valuable:

👉 **An edge.**

And now that you understand how it works...

👉 You just took that edge away.

THE TRAP SEQUENCE

Here's how it usually plays out:

You go in for a "quick test drive"
You like the car
You sit down "just to see numbers"
Time starts passing
You get hungry
You get tired
You start compromising

And before you know it...

👉 You're signing a deal you didn't fully control.

🔥 WHAT I PERSONALLY DO (AND WHY)

Let me be very clear about this.

When I'm buying a **brand-new car**...

👉 I do **not** test drive it.
👉 Not sometimes.
👉 Not "just to see."
👉 Not under any circumstances.

And here's why.

A brand-new car is going to:

Drive smoothly
Feel tight
Perform exactly as designed

There are no surprises.

There is nothing to "discover."

👉 The test drive is not for the car.
👉 It's for the dealership.

It exists to:

Get your driver's license
Start building your profile
Create emotional attachment
Move you further down their funnel

Once you understand that...

👉 The test drive loses its purpose.

I Already Know What I Want

By the time I walk into a dealership:

I've done my research
I've chosen the model
I understand the trims
I know the pricing landscape

I'm not there to "explore."

👉 I'm there to execute.

So driving the car adds nothing to my decision.

The Hidden Cost of "Just a Quick Drive"

Most people think:

"It's only five minutes."

But it's not.

That five-minute drive can:

Trigger data collection
Open the door to credit activity
Start the deal without you
Anchor you emotionally to the vehicle

And once that happens...

👉 You're no longer negotiating cleanly.

You're negotiating with attachment.

I Only Drive It Once

The only time I drive the car...

👉 Is when I'm leaving the dealership after closing the deal.

That's it.

Because at that point:

The numbers are done
The structure is locked
The control is mine

Now the drive actually means something.

And There's One More Reason

Let's say I *do* test drive it...

...and then during negotiation:

The numbers don't make sense
The dealer plays games
I decide to walk away

Now I've:

👉 Wasted time
👉 Created attachment
👉 Made it harder to leave

That's not a position I ever want to be in.

Important Distinction (Used vs. New)

Now—this is important.

This approach is specifically for:

👉 **Brand-new cars at large dealerships**

Used cars are different.

Condition varies
Wear and tear exists
Mechanical issues are possible

In those cases:

👉 A test drive can be useful.

Especially:

Private sellers
Small independent dealerships
Non-certified vehicles

Certified pre-owned vehicles?

👉 That becomes a gray area—use your judgment.

But for **brand-new vehicles**?

👉 There is no real upside to the test drive.
👉 Only leverage given away.

Final Thought

Most buyers think the test drive is part of the process.

It is.

👉 But not for the reason you think.

It's not about helping you decide.

☞ It's about helping them position you.

Once you see that clearly...

☞ You can choose to step out of that part of the game entirely.

And when you do...

☞ You walk into the negotiation cleaner, sharper, and fully in control.

Bottom Line

If you remember one thing from this section, remember this:

The test drive is not the goal.
Getting you there is the goal.

So you flip it.

☞ You control when you show up.
☞ You control what you discuss first.
☞ You control when and if test drive happens.

Not them.

Chapter 6

NEGOTIATE, NEGOTIATE & WIN

> "I did 20 years in the Ford dealership business. The best day to negotiate a deal is on the last day of the month. Enjoy."
>
> — @FACEYTX

Alright... this is where the book sharpens its teeth.

This chapter is not about "tips."

This is where the reader becomes dangerous.

There is a moment in every dealership experience where everything changes.

It's the moment you stop being a customer...

...and become a negotiator.

Most people never reach that moment.

They sit.
They listen.
They react.

They answer questions.
They follow the process.
They "see what happens."

And slowly...

they get guided into a deal.

THE TRUTH MOST PEOPLE DON'T WANT TO HEAR

You are not there to buy a car.

👉 You are there to negotiate a deal.

Those are not the same thing.

Buying is passive.

Negotiating is active.

Buying follows their structure.

Negotiating forces your structure.

THE REAL BATTLEFIELD

A dealership is not a store.

It's a controlled environment designed to do one thing:

👉 Extract as much money from you as possible.

Not because they are evil.

Because that is their business model.

They are trained.

You are not.

They do this every day.

You do this every few years.

That is the imbalance.

This chapter fixes that.

POSITIONING: WHO YOU ARE IN THE DEAL

Before numbers...

Before offers...

Before anything...

You need to understand your role.

There are only two types of buyers:

1. The Reactive Buyer

They:

Answer questions
Wait for offers
Adjust based on pressure
Focus on monthly payments

They are guided.

They are influenced.

They are controlled.

2. The Positioned Buyer

They:

Lead the conversation
Set expectations early
Stay focused on one number
Control pace and direction

They are not aggressive.

They are not rude.

They are simply...

👉 in control

Everything in this chapter is about becoming the second one.

MINDSET: THE GAME WITHIN THE GAME

Negotiation is not about numbers.

It's about control.

And control starts here:

👉 Your mindset

Rule #1 – Nothing Is Final Until You Sign

Not:

verbal agreements
not printed worksheets
not "manager approvals"

Only one thing matters:

👉 your signature

That means:

👉 you are always in control

Rule #2 – The Deal Is Never "Almost Done"

You will hear:

"We're almost there"
"Just one last step"
"Let's wrap this up"

No.

👉 The deal is not done until YOU decide it is

Rule #3 – Calm Beats Emotion

They want you:

excited
frustrated
tired
emotionally invested

Because:

- emotion makes you weak

Calm makes you **dangerous**.

CONTROL VS REACTION

This is the biggest shift in the entire book.

Most buyers:

- react

Great negotiators:

- control

What Reaction Looks Like

Salesperson:
"Here's the monthly payment..."

Buyer:
"Hmm... can we lower it?"

You just lost control.

What Control Looks Like

Salesperson:
"Here's the monthly payment..."

You:
"I'm not discussing monthly payments. What's the Out-the-Door price?"

Now you're in charge.

THE LASER FOCUS PRINCIPLE

There is only one objective:

☞ Get the car at the lowest possible Out-the-Door price

Everything else is noise.

They will try to distract you with:

monthly payments
trade-in value
add-ons
financing
timing
emotions

Your job is simple:

☞ Bring it back to the number

Every time.

THE REDIRECT TECHNIQUE

You will use this constantly:

"Yes, I understand...
☞ but let's get back to the total price."

Over and over again.

Until they realize:

☞ you cannot be moved

START THE NEGOTIATION BEFORE YOU WALK IN

This is where most people already lose.

They walk into a dealership...

☞ unprepared
☞ unknown
☞ unpositioned

You don't.

USE ONLINE QUOTES THE RIGHT WAY

Online quotes are not for buying the car.

They are for:

☞ identifying who plays games
☞ identifying who is transparent
☞ creating leverage before you arrive

Then:

communicate
ask questions
begin negotiation remotely

By the time you walk in:

☞ you are already in the game

PICK ONE DEALER – THEN CONTROL THE DEAL

Most buyers think:

👉 "I need to shop 5–10 dealerships"

That sounds smart.

It's not.

When dealers know you're shopping around:

👉 they hold back their best numbers

Instead:

choose one strong candidate
position yourself as a serious buyer
make it clear:

👉 "If the numbers are right, I'm buying today."

That changes everything.

THE AUTHORITY GAME (MANAGER TRICK)

You've seen it.

Salesperson says:

👉 "I have to talk to my manager."

They disappear.

They come back.

Repeat.

This is not negotiation.

This is theater.

Reality:

salesperson already knows the limits
manager already knows the numbers
the back-and-forth is designed to wear you down

YOUR MOVE

Option 1:
☞ Use the salesperson as your messenger

Option 2:
☞ Break the pattern

"Let's bring the manager here and finish this."

Once you recognize the tactic...

☞ it loses power

THE WAITING GAME

They disappear.

You wait.

Minutes turn into longer.

This is intentional.

Goal:

- ☞ make you uncomfortable
- ☞ make you anxious
- ☞ make you move first

YOUR COUNTER

Do nothing.

Literally.

Bring:

your phone
a book
work

Be relaxed.

Unbothered.

Even better:

- ☞ make THEM wait when they return

Now the pressure shifts.

THE GUILT TRAP

They might say:

"We can't make money at this price"
"We're losing on this deal"
"Help me out here"

No.

This is emotional manipulation.

Your response:

"I understand...
👉 but I'm focused on the price."

Stay neutral.

Stay steady.

THE "NO ROOM" LIE

They will say:

👉 "This is the best we can do"

Almost always...

👉 it's not

There is always a bottom line.

Your job:

👉 stay there longer than they expect

Because negotiation often comes down to one thing:

👉 who gets tired first

REBATES & FINANCING DISTRACTIONS

They will try to tie everything together:

"This price includes the rebate"
"You only get this if you finance"

Separate everything.

Rule:

👉 Negotiate the price first
👉 Apply incentives after

THE OFFER CHECK TRAP

They may say:

👉 "We need a deposit to continue"

No.

That is not required.

It is psychological pressure.

Rule:

👉 Never pay to negotiate

YOUR TWO ULTIMATE WEAPONS

You don't need tricks.

You don't need scripts.

You only need this:

1. Your Pen

👉 Only you sign

No one can force that.

2. Your Feet

👉 You can leave

At any moment.

That means:

👉 you always have control

THE SOFT WALKAWAY (ELITE MOVE)

This is where deals are won.

Not by arguing...

👉 but by leaving

But not aggressively.

Not emotionally.

Calmly:

"Looks like we're not there yet.
If things change, give me a call."

And you walk.

What happens next?

👉 "Wait... let me talk to my manager again."

That's the real negotiation.

EMOTION CONTROL = DEAL CONTROL

If you get:

angry
frustrated
impatient

You lose clarity.

And when you lose clarity...

👉 you lose money

Stay:

calm
patient
detached

Always remember:

👉 It's just a car

FINAL PRINCIPLE: STAY LOCKED IN

They will try:

distraction
delay
pressure
confusion

You do one thing:

👉 stay locked on the number

Over and over:

"Let's get back to the Out-the-Door price."

Until the deal breaks...

or they break.

Bottom Line

Negotiation is not about being smarter.

It's not about being aggressive.

It's not about winning arguments.

👉 It's about control

Control of:

your emotions
your focus
your timing
your decisions

Master that...

☞ and you will win far more deals than you lose

One Sentence to Remember

If you stay calm, stay focused, and stay willing to walk away...

☞ the dealership will eventually come to you.

PART III – HOW YOU TAKE CONTROL

Now You Flip the Game. Here's How You Win

Chapter 7

THE QUADRANT

Casino Trick REVEALED!

You are not negotiating one deal at the dealership.

You are negotiating **four deals at the same time**.

And that is exactly how they beat you.

THE FOUR QUADRANTS / THE FOUR SQUARE

Whether they draw it on paper, show it on a screen, or just juggle the numbers in conversation, the structure is always the same. The Quadrant (also known in the industry as the Four-Square method).

There are four variables:

Trade-in value (what they give you for your car)
Out-the-door price (OTD) of the vehicle
Cash down payment
Monthly payment

That's it.

That's the entire game.

And if you don't understand this structure, you are not negotiating...

👉 You are being **managed**.

WHY THIS WORKS SO WELL (AGAINST YOU)

The dealership does not want you thinking about four numbers.

They want you thinking about **one number**:

"How much do you want to pay per month?"

That's the trap.

Because the moment you focus on the monthly payment, you stop thinking like a buyer...

...and you start thinking like a **subscriber**.

THE $800 → $750 ILLUSION

Let's walk through a clean example so you can see exactly how this works.

Initial Setup

Trade-in: **$15,000**
OTD Price: **$50,000**
Down Payment: **$5,000**
Monthly Payment: **$800**

Now they ask you:

"Does $800 a month work for you?"

You say:

"I was really hoping to be closer to $750."

And that's when the magic trick begins.

THE "GOOD NEWS" RETURN

They disappear.

They go "talk to the manager."

They come back with a smile.

And then they say something like:

"Good news. We got you to $750."

And suddenly, everything feels like a win.

But here's what actually happened behind the scenes:

Trade-in: **$16,000** *(they "gave you more")*
Down Payment: **$7,000** *(you give them more)*
OTD Price: **still high (or even higher, hidden in structure)**
Monthly Payment: **$750**

You feel like you won.

But you didn't win anything.

👉 They just **moved money from one quadrant to another**.

THE SHELL GAME

This is not negotiation.

This is a **shell game**.

They move numbers around like this:

"We'll give you more for your trade" → but raise the price
"We'll lower your payment" → but extend the loan
"We'll make it work" → but increase your down payment

And because you are tired...

Because you've been there for hours...

Because you're hungry...

Because you just want to leave with a car...

👉 You accept the illusion.

THE REAL PROBLEM

The problem is not that they are adjusting numbers.

The problem is this:

You are trying to track four moving targets at the same time.

And you can't.

Nobody can.

That's why this system works so well.

THIS IS A CASINO

This is not a negotiation table.

This is a **casino table**.

And the game is designed so that:

You feel like you're making progress
You feel like you're getting closer
You feel like you're winning

But the house always knows the real numbers.

And you don't.

THE ONLY WAY TO WIN THIS GAME

You don't play four variables.

You reduce it to **one**.

THE ONLY NUMBER THAT MATTERS

Say this. Exactly like this:

"I want to negotiate one thing and one thing only."

Pause.

Then say:

"What is the out-the-door price of the vehicle?"

WHY THE OTD PRICE CHANGES EVERYTHING

The **Out-the-Door Price (OTD)** is the only number that matters because:

It includes **everything**
It cannot hide behind monthly payments

It cannot be manipulated with time
It cannot be disguised with emotion

It answers one simple question:

"If I wrote a check today, how much would I have to pay?"

That's it.

That's the real price of the car.

WHAT YOU MUST ASK FOR

Do not accept vague numbers.

Ask for a **full breakdown**:

Selling price
Discounts
Taxes
State fees
Dealer fees
Everything

And make it clear:

"I want to see this as if I'm paying cash."

Because once you remove financing...

👉 You remove the illusion.

SEQUENCE MATTERS

This is critical.

You do NOT discuss everything at once.

You go in this order:

Step 1 – Lock the OTD Price

Agree on the total cost of the vehicle.

Step 2 – Then discuss trade-in

Separate conversation.

Step 3 – Then discuss down payment

Your decision, not theirs.

Step 4 – Then financing

Only after everything else is locked.

WHY THEY HATE THIS

Because you just broke the system.

You took their four levers...

...and turned them into one.

Now:

They can't hide profit in your payment
They can't manipulate your emotions as easily
They can't move numbers around unnoticed

Now they actually have to give you a real deal.

WHAT WILL HAPPEN WHEN YOU DO THIS

Expect resistance.

They will try to pull you back into the monthly payment conversation.

They will say things like:

"Let's just see what works for you monthly"
"Most people prefer to focus on payment"
"We'll get there, don't worry about that"

Stay calm.

Repeat yourself.

"Let's agree on the out-the-door price first."

FINAL REALITY

You are going to get ripped off.

That hasn't changed.

But now...

👉 You control **how bad**.

THE TRUTH MOST PEOPLE NEVER REALIZE

Most people walk out of a dealership thinking:

"I got a good monthly payment."

Very few walk out knowing:

"I got a good deal."

And those are not the same thing.

Not even close.

The Bottom Line

If you remember nothing else from this chapter, remember this:

If you negotiate four numbers, you lose.

If you negotiate one number, you have a chance.

And that one number is:

The Out-the-Door Price.

When you understand this...

you are no longer just a customer.

👉 You are a problem they have to deal with.

HOW TO LOCK THE NUMBERS (YOUR HOMEWORK BEFORE YOU WALK IN)

Understanding the quadrant trick is step one.

Locking the numbers is how you **beat it**.

Because here's the truth:

If you walk into a dealership without doing your homework,
you are not negotiating...
you are guessing.

And guessing is expensive.

Step 1 – Lock the Out-the-Door Price (OTD)

Before you ever step into a dealership, you need to know one thing:

What is this car actually selling for in the real world?

Not what one dealership tells you.
Not what one salesperson suggests.

👉 **The market decides the real price.**

YOUR HOMEWORK

Search for the **exact same vehicle** in at least **five different dealerships**:

Same make
Same model
Same trim
As close as possible in features

Now look for:

OTD price (if available)
Or at least MSRP

Why This Matters

If four out of five dealerships show a similar MSRP...

👉 That's your baseline.

Now when one dealership tries to:

Add $1,000
Add $2,000
Add $3,000
Add $4,000

You'll see it immediately.

WATCH OUT FOR THIS TRICK

Some vehicles on the lot come with **extra add-ons**:

Digital rearview mirror
Protection packages
Accessories
Dealer-installed options

These are not always bad...

👉 But they are often **used as an excuse to increase the price**.

So when comparing:

Make sure you are comparing **apples to apples**
Understand what is included and what is not

THE GOAL

You walk into the dealership already knowing:

"This car should cost around THIS number."

Now you're not negotiating blindly.

👉 You're negotiating with **data**.

Step 2 – Lock Your Trade-In Value

Your trade-in is another place where money disappears quietly.

The dealership will try to:

Underprice your car
Justify it with "market conditions"
Then make it seem like they "helped you" later

YOUR HOMEWORK

Get at least **2 out of these 3 values**:

Carvana
Kelley Blue Book (KBB)
Another online appraisal tool

Enter:

Your VIN
Mileage

Condition
Features

WHAT YOU'RE LOOKING FOR

Not an exact number.

👉 A **range**.

If two platforms say:

$14,500
$15,200

Then you know:

Your car is worth around $14K–$15K

Why This Matters

Now when the dealership says:

"We can give you $12,000..."

You don't feel confused.

You don't feel unsure.

👉 You know.

And that changes everything.

Step 3 – Control the Down Payment

This is where most people give away power without realizing it.

The dealership will often ask early:

"How much are you putting down?"

That is not a casual question.

That is a **strategic question**.

THE RULE

Do NOT discuss your down payment yet.

Not until you have locked:

The OTD price
The trade-in value

Why?

Because the moment you tell them your down payment:

👉 They start adjusting the other quadrants around it.

They will use your own money to:

Lower your payment
Create fake "wins"
Restructure the deal in their favor

YOUR HOMEWORK

This one is simple:

👉 Decide your number privately.

Maybe it's $1,000
Maybe it's $5,000
Maybe it's $0

Only you know what you are comfortable with.

And you reveal that number **only when it benefits you**.

Step 4 – Take Control of Financing

Financing is another layer of the game.

And just like everything else...

👉 It can be used against you.

WHAT THEY WANT

They want you to use:

Their lenders
Their structure
Their terms

Because that's where they can:

Add profit
Adjust numbers
Control the monthly payment

AGAIN: THE CORRECT ORDER

This chapter becomes even more powerful once you understand the right order of operations.

Here is the order:

First, establish the out-the-door price.
Second, discuss the trade-in value.
Third, decide the down payment privately and only reveal it when it is strategically useful.
Fourth, handle financing.

That is the order.

Not the dealership's preferred order.
Your order.

The reason this matters is because every question they ask before step one is an attempt to rearrange the order in their favor.

They want the budget first.
They want the trade first.
They want the financing first.
They want your commitment first.

You want the OTD first.

That difference is the whole fight.

YOU DO NOT HAVE TO BE RUDE

Let me be clear about something important.

You do not have to be arrogant.

You do not have to be combative.
You do not have to walk in acting like a movie gangster.

In fact, that usually makes things worse.

What you need is not aggression.
What you need is calm repetition.

You smile.
You stay polite.
You stay brief.
You stay in control.

"Right now I just want to focus on the out-the-door price."
"Let's establish that first."
"We can talk about the rest after that."
"I haven't decided yet."
"It could go either way."
"I'll determine that once the full numbers make sense."

Those are strong answers because they are clean answers.

They do not overshare.
They do not apologize.
They do not invite extra traps.

They simply keep the conversation where it belongs.

YOUR HOMEWORK

Before you go in, check:

Your bank
A credit union
Any external lender

Get a **pre-approval** or at least an idea of your:

Interest rate (APR)
Loan terms

Why This Matters

Now you walk in with options.

If the dealership gives you:

A worse rate
Worse terms

👉 You don't need to accept it.

You already have a backup.

PUTTING IT ALL TOGETHER

Here is the correct order, always:

Lock the **OTD price**
Lock the **trade-in value**
Decide your **down payment (privately)**
Choose your **financing**

Final Truth

The dealership wins when:

You don't prepare

You rely on them for numbers
You negotiate emotionally

You win when:

You know the market
You know your car's value
You control your information

Bottom Line

The quadrant trick only works when you don't know your numbers.

Once you do...

👉 The game changes.

You are no longer reacting.

👉 You are controlling the deal.

Chapter 8

TRICKS, TIPS, HINTS & RECOMMENDATIONS

In this chapter, we will explore a number of tricks, tips and recommendations that are simply good to practice and know to give you an upper hand while unexpected unknowns appear during the process of buying a new (sometimes used) car at a dealership. If you have time, this is a good read and will give you some extra knowledge that might save you some extra hundreds or thousands of dollars. If you do not have the time, please make it. It is worth literally every penny.

FIVE QUESTIONS YOU SHOULD NEVER ANSWER

There are questions at the dealership that sound normal, harmless, even practical.

They are not.

They are not asked because the salesperson is curious.
They are not asked because the salesperson wants to help you.
They are not asked because the salesperson wants to save you time.

They are asked because every answer you give becomes a tool that can be used against you.

That is why this chapter matters.

A lot of buyers walk into a dealership thinking the danger begins when the paperwork comes out, when the monthly payment is shown, or when the finance manager starts pushing warranties and extra nonsense. But that is not when the danger begins. The danger begins much earlier. It begins with conversation. It begins with friendly questions. It begins with the salesperson trying to figure out how much information you are willing to hand over before you even know what the real deal is.

If you answer the wrong questions too early, you lose leverage before you ever start negotiating.

That is why there are five questions you should never answer directly, at least not at the beginning, and certainly not before you lock the out-the-door price.

The order matters.

The timing matters.

And your discipline matters.

Because the dealership wants to pull you into four negotiations at once: the car price, the trade-in, the down payment, and the monthly payment. The moment you allow that to happen, you are no longer controlling the deal. You are being moved around inside it.

So let's go one by one.

Question Number One: "What's Your Monthly Budget?"

This is probably the most common question in the whole dealership universe.

It sounds innocent.

It sounds reasonable.

It sounds almost helpful.

"What are you trying to stay around monthly?"

That question is a trap.

The reason it is a trap is simple: the dealership does not need to know your monthly budget in order to sell you a car. They need to know your monthly budget in order to shape the deal around the maximum pain you are willing to tolerate.

That is a big difference.

When they ask for your monthly budget, they are not asking, "What is the best total deal for you?" They are asking, "How much room do we have to play with?"

If you say, "I want to stay under $700 a month," you may think you are protecting yourself. You are not. You just told them the ceiling. You just told them the line they need to stay under while making money in every other area they can.

They can stretch the loan.
They can change the down payment.
They can move the trade-in value around.
They can increase the real price of the car while making the monthly payment look acceptable.

And suddenly you are sitting there happy because they got you to $695, while the total deal may still be terrible.

That is why your answer should not be your real budget.

Your answer should be something like this:

"I've already done my homework and I already know what fits into my budget. Right now I only want to focus on the out-the-door price."

That is the correct response.

You are not refusing to negotiate.
You are refusing to negotiate the wrong thing first.

That is a huge difference.

The monthly budget is private. It belongs to you. It is part of your planning, not part of their strategy. Once you reveal it too early, it becomes part of their strategy.

And remember something else: Once they start the conversation around monthly payment, they can guide you toward the car they want you to buy, not necessarily the car or the deal that is best for you.

So if they ask your monthly budget, bring the conversation back where it belongs:

The out-the-door price first.

Always first.

Question Number Two: "Do You Have a Trade-In?"

This one sounds even more harmless.

"Do you have a trade-in?"

What could possibly be wrong with that question?

A lot.

The problem is not that trade-ins are bad. The problem is that the dealership wants to combine your trade-in with the new car transaction as early as possible so they can blur the math and make the deal harder to follow.

The more parts they can combine, the harder it becomes for you to know where you are winning, where you are losing, and how badly you are getting ripped off.

If you say yes immediately, the dealership starts calculating the whole deal as one big tangled package. Now they can give you less on your trade, charge more for the car, and make it look balanced by tweaking the payment or pretending they "helped" you in one area.

That is exactly why the trade-in should be treated as irrelevant until the out-the-door price of the new vehicle is established.

Your response can be simple:

"I might. I haven't decided what I'm doing with that yet. Let's establish the out-the-door price first."
Or...
"My mother in-law is very interested in buying one of our vehicles for his youngest son. Let's just lock the out-the-door price first."

That is not dishonest. That is disciplined.

Because maybe you do have a trade-in.
Maybe you will use it.
Maybe you will sell it privately.
Maybe you will use Carvana.
Maybe you will keep it another week while you think about it.

The point is: they do not need that information yet.

The dealership wants to know about your trade-in early because it gives them another lever. It gives them another box to move numbers around in. It gives them another way to create the illusion that they are helping you when all they are really doing is restructuring the same money.

This is why you do your homework before you walk in. You should already have a realistic idea of what your vehicle is worth from tools like Kelley Blue Book and online offers. **Please** understand the importance of knowing what your trade is worth before you step into the building. If you know your range and they come in far below it, you will see the insult immediately.

But even if you know the value, do not let them drag the trade-in into the conversation too soon.

New car price first.
Trade-in second.

That order protects you.

Question Number Three: "Are You Financing or Paying Cash?"

Another innocent-sounding question.

Another trap.

"Are you financing or paying cash?"

What they are really asking is:
Where can we make our money?

If you say cash too early, they may lose interest in giving you the cleanest price, because they know they will not make as much on financing. If you say financing too early, they may start building the whole discussion around payment structure instead of real price. Either way, you are feeding them information before they have earned it.

The correct answer is:

"It could go either way. We can decide that after we establish the out-the-door price."

That answer protects you because it keeps your options open.

Maybe you already have preapproval from a bank.
Maybe you have a credit union rate in your pocket.
Maybe you are considering cash.
Maybe you will finance part and pay the rest later.

That is your business.

And the key phrase here is this: your financing decision should come after the vehicle price is locked, not before.

Because once they know how you plan to pay, they start calculating how they can shape the presentation of the deal around that method. If they know you are financing, they start moving quickly toward payment talk. If they know you are paying cash, they may try harder to bury profit in the vehicle price or dealer fees.

That is why you stay flexible.

Do not lie.
Do not ramble.
Do not explain your whole financial life.

Just keep the conversation on track.

"We can talk about that after we establish the out-the-door price."

It may sound repetitive.

Good.

This is one of those times in life where being repetitive is a form of intelligence.

Question Number Four: "What's the Most You'll Pay?"

This is one of the boldest questions they ask because it is so nakedly self-serving.

"What's the max you'll pay?"

Think about what they are really asking.

They are asking you to negotiate against yourself.

They are asking you to announce your ceiling before they announce their floor.

That makes no sense for you.

If you are selling something, you want the highest number.
If you are buying something, you want the lowest number.

That is basic reality.

So when they ask, "What's the most you'll pay?" the best mental answer is:

"What's the least you'll take?"

That is the true counterweight to their question.

Now, you do not have to say it with attitude. You do not have to be rude. But you do have to understand the game. They want your maximum because your maximum gives them permission to stop negotiating early and build the deal around the outer edge of your comfort zone.

That is why you do not answer that question directly.

You bring it back again:

"Let's first establish the out-the-door price and then we can see whether the numbers make sense."

That answer is calm.
It is intelligent.
And it refuses to give away leverage.

The truth is, every dealership wants to discover two things as quickly as possible: your emotional attachment and your financial ceiling. Once they know both, they can work on you. Your job is to reveal neither of them too early.

And this matters even more when you are tired. Dealerships are experts at the battle of who gets tired first. They know that after hours of talking, waiting, sitting, and reworking numbers, many buyers just want closure. That is exactly why you must not hand them your maximum. Once they know it, exhaustion does the rest.

Question Number Five: "If I Can Get You This Number, Will You Buy Today?"

This is one of the slickest questions because it creates fake momentum.

"If I can get you another $1,000 for your trade, will you buy today?"
"If I can get your payment down to this number, will you buy today?"
"If I can make the manager happy and get this approved, will you buy today?"

This sounds like progress.

Sometimes it even feels flattering, like the salesperson is fighting for you.

But what this question is really doing is trying to get a commitment from you before the entire deal is clean, complete, and understood.

That is a problem.

Because maybe the one number improved but three others quietly got worse. Maybe they lowered the payment but extended the loan. Maybe they raised the trade-in but increased the down payment. Maybe they cut one fee and added two others.

That is why your answer should be:

"I don't know. Let's first work out the out-the-door price, and then we'll see whether the full deal makes sense."

That answer protects you from premature commitment.

Never promise to buy based on one moving part inside a deal that contains multiple moving parts.

That is like agreeing to marry someone because they have nice shoes.

You do not commit based on one appealing detail. You commit when the whole thing makes sense.

And remember this: once they get a verbal "yes" out of you, even a soft one, they start acting as if the sale is emotionally done. Now you are not just negotiating numbers; you are trying to undo a psychological commitment that they will keep using against you.

So do not give them that commitment early.

Let the whole deal earn the yes.

Why All Five Questions Exist

At this point, you may notice that the answer sounds repetitive.

Good.

That repetition is the point.

Because all five questions are really designed to do the same thing: drag you away from the out-the-door price and into a swamp of side issues before the main number is settled.

That is why your answer keeps coming back to the same place.

The OTD.

The real total.

The price as if you were writing a check today.

That is the anchor.

That is the number that keeps the conversation honest.

Or at least as honest as a dealership conversation can become.

If you let them lead with monthly budget, trade-in, financing method, max price, and same-day commitment, they are building a mental maze around you. If you keep redirecting the discussion back to the OTD, you are removing walls from the maze.

That is how you stay clear.

That is how you stay hard to manipulate.

That is how you stop getting ripped off that bad.

Final Thought

The dealership is not just selling you a car.

They are trying to manage your attention.

That is what these five questions are really about.

If they can control your attention, they can control the pace.
If they can control the pace, they can control the pressure.
If they can control the pressure, they can control the deal.

So do not answer these five questions the way they want.

Answer them in a way that protects your leverage.

And if your response starts sounding repetitive, remember this:

That is because the truth at the dealership is repetitive.

You want one thing first and one thing only.

The out-the-door price.

Everything else comes after.

FIVE ACTIONS SMART CAR SHOPPERS TAKE

The Habits That Separate Buyers from Targets

Most people walk into a dealership hoping for a good deal.

Smart buyers don't hope.

👉 They prepare.

Because by the time you step into a dealership, the game has already started.

And if you haven't done the work beforehand...

👉 You are already behind.

The following five actions are what separate:

👉 Someone who gets a deal
from
👉 Someone who gets worked

These are not advanced tricks.

They are simple.

But they are powerful—if you actually do them.

1. Know How Long the Car Has Been on the Lot

Every car sitting on a dealership lot has a clock on it.

Not a visible one.

👉 But a very real one.

The longer a car sits...

👉 The more motivated the dealership becomes to move it.

This is called:

👉 **Days on Lot**

A vehicle that has been sitting for:

5 days → no urgency
15 days → normal
30+ days → attention
60+ days → pressure
90+ days → problem

At that point, the dealership is thinking:

"We need to move this."

That's your opportunity.

Why This Matters

Dealerships:

Pay interest to keep inventory
Want fresh inventory flowing
Don't like stagnant cars

So the longer it sits...

👉 The more flexible they become

What You Should Do

Ask:

"How long has this vehicle been on the lot?"

They may answer directly.

They may not.

Either way:

👉 You just signaled something important

👉 You are not guessing.

2. Know Brand Incentives Before They Tell You

Manufacturers often offer:

Rebates
Special financing
Lease deals
Loyalty programs
Bonus incentives

And here's the important part:

👉 These incentives come from the manufacturer—not the dealership

Why This Matters

Dealerships sometimes present incentives like this:

"We're giving you a $2,000 discount."

When in reality:

👉 That discount came from the manufacturer

Not them.

What You Should Do

Before you walk in:

👉 Go to the brand's official website

Look for:

Current offers
Rebates
Special financing
Regional incentives

Now when you walk in:

👉 You already know what exists

You're not waiting for them to "offer" it.

3. Do Real Market Research (Not Guessing)

Walking into a dealership without market knowledge is like:

👉 Walking into a poker game without knowing the rules

You might win.

But probably not.

What Market Research Means

You should know:

Typical selling price for the vehicle
How it compares across dealerships
Whether it's in high demand or not
Whether inventory is tight or plentiful

Why This Matters

Because pricing is not random.

👉 It's influenced by the market

If a car is:

In high demand → less discount
Sitting longer → more flexibility
Widely available → competitive pricing

What You Should Do

Check:

Multiple dealership listings
Online pricing tools
Inventory levels
Variations in pricing for the same model

Now when you negotiate:

☞ You are not guessing

☞ You are referencing reality

4. Get Insurance Quotes Before You Buy

This is one of the most overlooked steps.

And one of the most expensive mistakes.

The Problem

You buy the car.

You feel good.

You finalize everything.

Then you call your insurance...

☞ And the premium is way higher than expected.

Now what?

You already bought the car.

Why This Happens

Insurance is based on:

Vehicle type
Repair costs
Theft rates
Safety ratings
Driver profile

Some cars cost significantly more to insure than others.

Even if the price of the car is similar.

What You Should Do

Before you commit:

☞ Call your insurance company

Or:

☞ Get an online quote

Takes a few minutes.

Saves you from surprises.

5. Know Your Budget—and Stick to It

This one sounds obvious.

But it's where most people lose control.

. . .

The Reality

The dealership will try to:

Stretch your payment
Adjust your terms
Make numbers "work"

And slowly...

👉 Move you beyond your original comfort zone

Why This Happens

Because once you're there:

You've invested time
You've built emotional attachment
You want the car

And your budget becomes...

👉 flexible

What You Should Do

Before you go in:

👉 Decide your real number

Monthly comfort
Total comfort
Down payment limits

And then:

👉 Stick to it like Velcro

No adjustments.

No exceptions.

No emotional upgrades.

Final Truth

Smart car shoppers don't rely on the dealership to educate them.

👉 They walk in already informed.

Because the dealership is not there to protect your money.

👉 You are.

Bottom Line

These five actions don't make you aggressive.

They make you:

👉 prepared

- aware
- harder to manipulate

One Sentence to Remember

The best deals don't happen at the dealership...

- They start before you walk in.

FIVE QUESTIONS THAT INSTANTLY PUT YOU IN CONTROL (AND DEALERS HATE!)

What Smart Buyers Ask That Dealers Wish You Wouldn't

There are questions the dealership wants you to answer.

And then there are questions...

👉 They hope you never ask.

Because the moment you ask the right questions:

The structure changes
The tone changes
The control shifts

And suddenly...

👉 You are no longer the easy customer

You are the informed one.

1. "Can I Get the Out-the-Door Price?"

This is the most important question you can ask.

And one of the most uncomfortable for them.

Why They Don't Like It

Because it removes:

👉 confusion
👉 manipulation
👉 hidden movement

The Out-the-Door (OTD) price shows:

Vehicle price
Fees
Taxes
Add-ons
Everything

👉 One number
👉 Full transparency

Why It Matters

It allows you to:

Compare deals across dealerships
Spot inflated fees
Identify unnecessary add-ons

It turns:

👉 a messy deal
into
👉 a clean number

What You Do Next

Once you see the breakdown, you say:

"I don't want these add-ons. Remove them."

And now...

👉 You're negotiating for real

2. "Remove the Add-Ons—I Don't Want Them."

This is not a polite request.

This is a decision.

Why This Matters

Dealerships often add:

Protection packages
Appearance kits
Nitrogen tires
Tracking systems
"Mandatory" upgrades

These are:

👉 massive profit centers

What Happens When You Push Back

Their mood may change.

That's normal.

Because:

👉 You just reduced their profit

How to Say It (Correctly)

Not:

"Can you remove this?"

Say:

"I need you to remove this."

Because "can you" gives them an out.

👉 "We can't."

"I need you to" forces the conversation.

Important Reality

You may need to ask:

👉 more than once
👉 calmly
👉 firmly

And if needed...

👉 walk away

3. "Can I See the Buyer's Order Before I Come In?"

This one is powerful.

And uncomfortable for them.

What a Buyer's Order Does

It shows:

Final agreed price
Fees
Structure
Total deal

👉 In writing

Why They Don't Like This

Because once it's written:

👉 It's harder to change later

And here's the truth:

This happens more often than people think:

You agree to numbers remotely
You show up
Suddenly... things change

What This Question Does

It eliminates:

- last-minute surprises
- "misunderstandings"
- quiet price increases

It turns on the light in a dark room.

Now you can see everything.

4. "I Have My Own Financing—That Won't Be a Problem, Right?"

This is a big one.

Why They Don't Like It

Because financing is:

- one of their biggest profit centers

When you bring your own financing:

- You reduce their ability to mark up your rate

What Actually Happens

If you have a strong pre-approval:

- They may try to match or beat it

Why?

Because even a smaller profit is:

- better than no profit

What This Does for You

It gives you:

Leverage
Control
Options

You are no longer dependent.

Important Strategy

You don't need to reveal this immediately.

But when you do...

- It changes everything

5. "Can I See the Invoice—or Your Cost Breakdown?"

This question goes deeper.

And yes...

- it makes them uncomfortable

. . .

What You're Asking For

You're asking to see:

What they paid for the car
What's built into it
What costs are attached

Why This Matters

Because pricing is not always transparent.

Even invoice pricing can include:

Hidden incentives
Dealer adjustments
Internal credits

So when you ask:

👉 You're signaling something important

👉 You are not negotiating blindly

Advanced Version (Very Niche)

You can ask for:

Pre-delivery inspection records

Repair orders
Internal cost breakdowns

This is advanced.

And yes...

👉 They may look at you like you work in the industry

That's fine.

Bonus (Used Cars Only)

"Can I Get a Pre-Purchase Inspection?"

If you're buying used:

👉 This is non-negotiable

Why It Matters

A third-party mechanic gives you:

Unbiased insight
Real condition
Hidden issues

Red Flag

If they say:

"No, we don't allow that"

- You don't buy that car

Simple.

Final Truth

Dealerships make money when:

- You don't ask questions

They lose control when:

- You ask the right ones

Bottom Line

You don't need to be aggressive.

You don't need to be confrontational.

You just need to be:

- clear
- direct
- consistent

One Sentence to Remember

You don't take control of the deal by answering questions...

☞ You take control by asking the right ones.

THE 5 LIES CAR DEALERS STILL USE

(And how to recognize them before they cost you thousands)

There are phrases in a dealership that sound normal... even reasonable.

But once you know what they really mean, you'll never hear them the same way again.

Think of these as **audio red flags**.
Not what you see... what you hear.

Because the moment one of these comes out of a salesperson's mouth, you're no longer having a conversation.

You're being worked.

Let's break them down.

► 1. "The factory made us add a market adjustment."

Translation:
"We decided to charge you more because we can."

This one is dressed up to sound official.
Like it's coming from some higher authority.

The "factory."

It isn't.

The manufacturer does **not** force dealers to add markups.
That decision is made at the dealership level.

So when you hear this, understand what's really happening:

They're trying to remove themselves from responsibility.

"It's not us... it's them."

No.
It's them.

2. "The bank requires an extended warranty to approve the loan."

This one isn't just misleading.

It's flat-out false.

Banks care about:

your credit
your income
the loan structure

They do **not** require extended warranties.

Ever.

This line exists for one reason only:

To bundle a high-profit product into your deal
and make it feel mandatory.

If you hear this, you're not being informed.

You're being pressured.

3. "All our cars come with this package."

This is the classic:

paint protection
nitrogen tires
fabric guard
random add-ons you didn't ask for

And the key word they use is:

"All."

Because "all" sounds final.
Like there's no way around it.

But here's the truth:

There is always a way around it.

Especially if:

the car is being ordered
or the package hasn't been installed yet

This isn't policy.

It's positioning.

4. "There's no profit in this car."

This one might be the boldest.

Because it asks you to believe something that almost never exists:

A dealership selling a car... for nothing.

Let's be clear:

There is always profit.

Maybe not where you think.
Maybe not in the obvious place.

But it's there.

Between:

holdbacks
incentives
financing
add-ons

Dealerships don't survive on charity.

So when you hear this line, understand:

You're being asked to stop negotiating.

5. "If you don't buy it, someone else will."

This is not information.

This is pressure.

It's designed to trigger:

urgency
fear of loss
emotional decision-making

And once emotion takes over, logic disappears.

Sometimes it's true.

Most of the time, it's not.

Either way, it doesn't matter.

Because your decision should never be based on:
what someone else *might* do.

Bonus Red Flag

"What do I have to do to earn your business?"

This one sounds polite.

Professional.

Even respectful.

It's not.

It's a reset button.

It shifts the conversation from:

facts
numbers
structure

...into something vague and emotional.

Now you're negotiating feelings instead of terms.

And that's exactly where they want you.

Because once you answer that question,
you've just told them how to close you.

If a sales person needs to ask: "What do I have to do to earn your business?", that is because she already lost it the moment she asked the question.

🧠 Final Thought

Most people walk into a dealership looking for:

the best price
the best deal
the right car

But the real advantage isn't in what you ask.

It's in what you **recognize**.

Because once you can hear these lines for what they are...

You stop reacting.

And you start controlling the conversation.

7 FEES SMART BUYERS REFUSE TO PAY

The Charges That Quietly Inflate Your Deal

There's a moment in every car deal when the worksheet finally shows up.

And suddenly...

The clean, simple price you thought you were negotiating...

👉 turns into a list.

A long list.

Of fees.

Charges.
Packages.
Add-ons.
Mystery items.

Some look official.
Some sound legitimate.
Some are just confusing enough that you don't question them.

And that's exactly the point.

Because the goal is not to make the fees obvious.

👉 The goal is to make them *accepted.*

So let's strip the illusion away.

Below are **seven of the most common fees smart buyers either reject, question, or negotiate aggressively**—based on real-world dealership practices.

1. Freight / Destination Fee (The Double Charge)

This one sounds legitimate.

Freight.
Destination.
Shipping.

It sounds like the cost to bring the vehicle to the dealership.

But here's the truth:

👉 It is already included in the MSRP.

That means:

👉 You've already paid for it once.

So when you see it again as a separate line item?

👉 That's a duplicate charge.

In some cases, dealerships even "balance" it out with a fake discount to make it look legitimate.

That's not pricing.

👉 That's gamesmanship.

❗ **Important:** A legitimate manufacturer destination charge already printed on the factory window sticker is different from a dealership adding additional freight, prep, transport, or handling charges on top of it. The problem is not the original manufacturer destination fee—the problem is duplicate or inflated dealership-added versions of it.

2. Dealer Prep / PDI (Already Paid For)

This one might be the most absurd.

Dealer Prep.
Pre-Delivery Inspection (PDI).
Vehicle Preparation.

It sounds like necessary work before you take the car home.

But here's what they don't tell you:

👉 The manufacturer already pays the dealership for this.

That's part of the agreement.

So when you see a charge like:

\$800
\$1,200
\$1,700+

👉 You are being charged for something that has already been paid for.

That is not a service.

👉 That is pure margin.

3. "Mystery Fees" (Undefined Charges Like PIPA)

These are the most dangerous.

Because they are vague.

They have names like:

PIPA
Processing Fee #2
Administrative Charge
"Dealer Program Fee"

And when you ask what they are?

You get a vague answer.

Or no answer.

Here's the rule:

👉 If you don't understand it, you don't accept it.

And remember:

👉 **If it's taxable... it's negotiable.**

That one line alone can save you hundreds—or thousands.

Because if it's being taxed, it's being treated as part of the selling price.

Which means:

👉 It's not fixed
👉 It's not required
👉 It can be reduced or removed

4. Reconditioning Fees (Used Car Trap)

You'll see this mostly on used cars.

Reconditioning
Inspection
Vehicle Prep
Lot Ready Fee

And it will look like:

$500
$1,000
$3,000+

Here's the truth:

That cost is already built into the price of the car.

When a dealer buys a used vehicle:

They factor in repairs
They factor in transport
They factor in cleanup

Then they price the car accordingly.

So when they add it again as a line item?

That's double charging.

5. Add-Ons Disguised as "Standard Equipment"

These are everywhere.

And they come with fancy names.

You'll see things like:

Nitrogen-filled tires

Window etching
Paint protection
Pinstripes
Security systems
Protection coatings

And they'll often already be installed.

Which creates pressure.

Because now it feels like:

"Well... it's already on the car..."

But here's the reality:

👉 These are optional.
👉 These are overpriced.
👉 These are profit centers.

And here's the key:

👉 You do not pay list price.

If you want them, negotiate them.

If you don't want them, remove them.

Simple.

6. Bundled "Packages" (The $2,000 Mystery Box)

These are the sneakiest.

Because they combine multiple small items into one big number.

You'll see something like:

"Safety & Security Package" — $2,000

Sounds important.

Sounds valuable.

But when you ask what's inside?

It's usually:

Low-value accessories
Overpriced add-ons
Things you didn't ask for

And here's the key question:

👉 "What exactly is included?"

Then:

👉 "Can you remove it?"

Because just because it's bundled...

👉 doesn't mean it's required.

7. The Doc Fee (The One You Don't Remove—But Offset)

This one is different.

Because unlike the others:

👉 You probably won't get it removed.

Dealers will tell you:

"We have to charge everyone the same doc fee."

And in many cases, they're right—at least structurally.

But here's the strategy:

👉 You don't fight the doc fee directly.

👉 You offset it.

If the doc fee is $500...

👉 You negotiate $500 off the selling price.

Same result.

Different approach.

Because at the end of the day:

👉 It's still a profit center.

The Pattern You Need to See

All of these fees follow the same pattern:

They sound official
They appear late
They rely on confusion
They assume you won't push back

And most importantly:

👉 They are rarely questioned

. . .

Remember: Where You Fight These Fees (This Matters)

This is critical. Like we already mentioned earlier in this book...

You do NOT fight these in the finance office.

👉 You fight these on the sales floor.

Because:

Sales controls the price
Sales controls the car
Sales controls the add-ons

The finance office?

👉 They sell different products.

So if you wait too long...

👉 You lose leverage.

Bottom Line

Not every fee is fake.

But many are:

👉 Inflated
👉 Duplicated
👉 Optional
👉 Or completely unnecessary

And every fee you don't question...

👉 becomes money you don't get back.

One Sentence to Remember

If you don't understand a fee...

👉 You don't pay it.

TRICK: NEVER SAY YOU'RE PAYING CASH TOO EARLY 💸

A Smart Trick That Can Save You Thousands

Most people think telling the dealership they are paying cash is a power move.

It sounds strong.
It sounds responsible.
It sounds like leverage.

But in many cases...

👉 it does the opposite.

It actually weakens your negotiating position.

And that surprises people because on the surface, cash feels like king.

In real estate, maybe.

At a dealership? Not necessarily.

Because the dealership does not just want to sell you a car.

👉 They want to make money on the **whole deal**.

And one of the easiest places for them to make extra money is financing. Dealerships do not make the bulk of their profit from the new car itself; a large portion of profit comes from finance and insurance products, accessories, service fees, and other back-end opportunities.

That changes everything.

Why Cash Can Actually Hurt You

Let's say you walk into a dealership and announce this proudly:

"Just so you know, I'm paying cash."

You think you just showed strength.

What the dealership hears is something very different:

"One of our biggest profit centers just disappeared."

That matters.

Because once they know they will not make money through financing, they may become:

Less flexible on price
Less willing to remove junk fees
Less willing to take off accessories
Less motivated to give you their best deal

Why?

Because now they have fewer ways to make money on you.

And when a dealership feels boxed in on profit, it often tries to recover that lost profit somewhere else.

Maybe through:

Add-ons
Accessories
Higher selling price
More stubborn out-the-door numbers
Less room to negotiate

That is why telling them too early that you are paying cash is often a mistake. Many cash buyers "shoot themselves in the foot" during the negotiation phase because they remove financing profit from the table before the deal is structured.

The Better Strategy

The smarter move is simple:

👉 **Do not reveal that you plan to pay cash during the sales negotiation.**

Let the dealership believe financing is possible.

That does not mean you have to commit to financing through them.

It means you do not take away their incentive too early.

You keep the deal alive.

You keep them interested.

You keep them motivated to sharpen the pencil.

Because as long as they think they may make money in the finance office, they are often more willing to work with you on:

Selling price
OTD price
Certain add-ons
Certain fee reductions
Overall flexibility

That is the trick.

Not deception for the sake of deception.

Strategy.

Why This Works

Dealerships often make money on financing in two ways.

First, they may get a **flat fee or commission** from placing the loan.

Second, and more importantly, they may mark up the interest rate above the lender's real approval rate. The dealership can receive a buy rate from the lender, then add extra points on top as the sell rate, creating profit through the spread.

So if the dealership believes financing is still possible, they may think:

"We can give a little more on the front end because we might recover it on the back end."

That helps you.

The moment you tell them cash is your plan, that potential disappears.

And now they are negotiating with less hope of back-end profit.

That usually does not make them nicer.

The Smartest Version of the Trick

Now let's go one step deeper.

If you truly have the cash to buy the car outright, one smart strategy is this:

Negotiate the deal without announcing you are paying cash
Let financing remain on the table

Ideally use outside financing or a pre-approval from a bank or credit union
Complete the deal
Pay off the loan very quickly with your cash

This way, you preserve your negotiating leverage during the sales process, but still end up owning the vehicle without carrying long-term debt.

That is the real move.

You can still get the benefit of negotiating as a financed buyer, then pay off the balance afterward and effectively end up paying cash anyway.

But There's a Big Warning

This only works if:

👉 **There is no prepayment penalty.**

That matters.

Because some loans charge you a penalty if you pay them off too early.

So before you do anything like this, you must verify:

Whether the loan has an early payoff penalty
Whether there are any finance charges or clauses that punish rapid payoff
Whether the lender allows early payoff without nonsense

If there is a penalty, this strategy may not be worth it.

If there is no penalty, then it can be an excellent move.

That's not a small detail.

That's the whole key.

Use a Bank or Credit Union if Possible

If you are going to take the short-term financing route and pay it off quickly, it is often smarter to use:

Your bank
A credit union
Another outside lender you trust

Why?

Because that gives you:

A known interest rate
Cleaner terms
Greater transparency
Stronger leverage going into the dealership

Using pre-approval and outside financing gives you negotiating power because now the dealership must match or beat something real rather than sell you a mystery rate.

And if you do decide to finance through the dealership temporarily, at least you are walking in informed.

Not blind.

Do Not Wait Too Long to Pay It Off

Should you pay the loan off in 30 to 45 days?

☞ That is probably too long.

Why?

Because interest is accruing daily.

So if your real goal is to use financing only as a temporary strategy, then waiting a full month or more just adds unnecessary interest cost.

A more efficient move is to wait until the loan is fully booked by the lender—often around **7 to 10 days**—then call for the payoff amount and pay it immediately. That way, you still complete the strategy, but you reduce how much interest you pay along the way.

That is a very practical detail, and it matters.

Because if you are trying to save money, why give away extra days of interest for no reason?

☞ Negotiate car-related fees, accessories, and add-ons on the sales floor, not in the finance office

That includes things like:

Dealer-added accessories
Prep charges
Appearance packages
Floor-installed add-ons
Junk fees attached to the vehicle itself

Why?

Because those belong to the sales side of the deal.

By the time you reach the finance office, the finance manager usually controls:

The loan paperwork
Warranty products
GAP
protection services
finance-related products

That is a different world.

So if you want something removed from the car deal itself, do that earlier.

Not later.

That timing distinction is important.

If you wait until the finance office to fight the wrong battle, you are negotiating in the wrong room.

What This Trick Is Really About

This trick is not about being sneaky.

It is about understanding incentives.

The dealership behaves differently depending on how it expects to make money.

If it believes there is profit in financing, it may work harder to earn your deal.

If it knows there is no financing profit and no back-end opportunity, it may tighten up immediately.

So your goal is not to impress them with cash.

Your goal is to:

👉 get the best overall deal.

That's the difference.

Too many people want the emotional satisfaction of saying:

"I'm paying cash."

But emotional satisfaction is not the same thing as negotiating leverage.

At the dealership, what feels powerful is not always what is powerful.

When You Finally Reveal the Cash

So when do you reveal it?

At the end.

After:

The OTD price is locked
The fee structure is clear
The accessories have been addressed
The deal is where you want it

Then—and only then—you decide how to pay.

If you still want to pay cash outright, that is your call.

If you want to use short-term financing and pay it off in 7 to 10 days, that is also your call.

But either way, you make that move **after** the negotiation is finished.

Not before.

Bottom Line

If you tell the dealership too early that you are paying cash, you may accidentally reduce your own negotiating power.

That is the trap.

A smarter move is to keep financing alive during negotiation, lock the best deal you can, and then decide how to pay at the end.

And if you do use a loan temporarily, make sure:

there is no prepayment penalty
the payoff terms are clear
and you pay it off quickly once the loan is booked

Because the goal is not to impress the dealership.

👉 The goal is to spend less money.

One Sentence to Remember

Cash feels powerful.

But at the dealership, silence about cash is often more powerful.

Chapter 9

THE FINANCE OFFICE: THE FINAL TRAP

The Big Fish Interrogates You 🐡

SECTION 1 – THE ROOM WHERE THEY FINISH YOU

You made it.

You chose the car.
You negotiated.
You went back and forth.
You said no.
You said maybe.
You stayed longer than you wanted.

And now...

👉 You think the hard part is over.

It's not.

The Most Dangerous Room in the Dealership

After everything feels "done," they say something like:

"Great, we're all set. Let's head into the finance office to finalize everything."

That sounds harmless.

It sounds like paperwork.

It sounds like the last step.

It's not.

👉 It's the most dangerous room in the entire dealership.

You Walk In Tired

By the time you sit in that chair:

You've been there for hours
You're mentally drained
You're hungry
You just want to leave
You want the process to be over

And most importantly:

👉 You already feel like you "won something"

Even if you didn't.

That feeling is exactly what they're waiting for.

New Person. Same Game. Different Strategy.

Now you're sitting across from someone new.

Not the salesperson.

👉 The finance manager.

This person is different.

Less friendly

More serious
More controlled
More precise

But make no mistake:

👉 This person is not there to process paperwork.

This person is there to make money.

The Final Opportunity

The dealership already made money on:

The car
The trade-in
The structure of the deal

But this...

👉 This is their final opportunity to make more.

And they take it seriously.

The Weapon: Fear

The salesperson used:

Energy
Conversation
Time
Pressure

The finance manager uses something else:

👉 Fear.

How It Begins

It starts casually.

"Just a few quick things before we wrap this up."

Then:

"Do you want to protect your investment?"

Then:

"Most of our customers choose this..."

Then:

"I don't want to scare you, but..."

That's your signal.

Because yes...

👉 They are trying to scare you.

The Add-On Machine Parade

Here's what usually comes next:

- Extended warranties
- Gap insurance
- Payment protection
- "Bumper-to-bumper" coverage
- Loss protection

- Maintenance plans

Each one comes with a pitch.

Each one sounds reasonable.

Each one sounds small.

The Monthly Trap Returns

They don't say:

"This will cost you $1,200."

They say:

"It's only $9 more a month."

Or:

"That's just $0.30 a day."

Sounds like nothing.

Feels like nothing.

But it's not nothing.

The Illusion of Safety

They frame everything as protection:

"What if something breaks?"

"What if you lose your job?"
"What if something happens?"

And suddenly, you're not thinking about:

👉 Cost

You're thinking about:

👉 Risk

This Is Not About Logic

At this point, you are tired.

You don't want to do math.

You don't want to calculate totals.

You don't want to restart the negotiation.

You just want to finish.

That's why this works.

The Pressure Without Pressure

They don't yell.

They don't rush you.

They don't push aggressively.

They just sit there calmly and say:

"It's up to you."

But everything around that sentence is designed to push you toward yes.

The Quiet Reality

Let's be fair for a moment.

Some of these products:

Can be useful
Can make sense
Can help in certain situations

This is not about saying everything is bad.

This is about understanding:

👉 The context is not neutral.

You are being sold to...

👉 At your weakest moment.

The Math You Must Do (Even When Tired)

Whenever you hear:

"Only $X more per month..."

You must immediately think:

👉 "Multiply that by 60... or 72..."

Because:

$9 × 72 = $648
$30 × 72 = $2,160

That's not small anymore.

The Final Trap

This is the final trap because:

You already committed emotionally
You already invested time
You already see yourself leaving with the car

And now they add:

👉 Small decisions that turn into big money

The Most Important Skill Here

You don't need to argue.

You don't need to debate.

You don't need to prove anything.

You just need one simple skill:

👉 The ability to say "No" calmly.

How to Say No (Correctly)

Not aggressive.

Not defensive.

Just clear:

"No, I'm good."
"I'm not interested in that."
"I'll pass on that."
"I've already made my decision."

And then...

👉 Silence.

Final Truth

The finance office is not where they finalize the deal.

👉 It's where they try to improve it... for themselves.

Bottom Line

If you walk into that room thinking:

"This is just paperwork"

You will leave having paid more than you needed to.

If you walk into that room knowing:

"This is the final sales pitch"

👉 You stay in control.

SECTION 2 – THE INTEREST RATE SCAM

Financing: The Invisible Profit Machine

You think the dealership makes money when they sell you the car.

They do.

But that's not where they make the **easiest money**.

The easiest money...
👉 is when they finance you.

And most people have absolutely no idea how it works.

"Never finance through the car dealership."

The Setup: Indirect Lending

When you walk into a dealership and say:

"Yeah, I'll just finance through you guys."

You just entered a system called: 👉 **Indirect Lending**

Buy Rate vs. Sell Rate: The Hidden Spread

There is a number in your car loan that you will never see.

It is not printed clearly.
It is not explained openly.
And in most cases...

👉 It is never mentioned at all.

But it directly determines how much extra money you pay.

The Two Rates You Need to Know

When you finance through a dealership, there are actually **two interest rates** involved:

☞ **The Buy Rate**
☞ **The Sell Rate**

THE BUY RATE

The **Buy Rate** is:

☞ The interest rate the bank gives to the dealership

This is the *real* cost of the money.

This is what the bank is willing to lend at based on:

Your credit
Your financial profile
The structure of the loan

THE SELL RATE

The **Sell Rate** is:

☞ The interest rate the dealership gives to YOU

And here's the key:

☞ The dealership is allowed to increase the Buy Rate.

The Spread (Where They Make Money)

The difference between these two rates is called:

👉 **The Spread**

And that spread is:

👉 **Pure profit for the dealership**

How Much Do They Mark It Up?

Typically:

👉 **1% to 3% higher than the Buy Rate**

So if the bank approves you at:

👉 5% (Buy Rate)

The dealership may offer you:

👉 6.5% or 7% (Sell Rate)

Why This Matters (A Lot)

At first glance, 2% doesn't sound like much.

But over time...

👉 It becomes thousands of dollars.

Real Example

Let's say:

Loan: $50,000
Term: 72 months

At **5%**:

Total interest ≈ **$7,000**

At **7%**:

Total interest ≈ **$10,000+**

👉 That's **$3,000 extra**

For the same car.
Same loan.
Same you.

What Did You Get for That Extra $3,000?

Nothing.

No upgrade.
No better car.
No better service.

👉 Just a higher number.

WHY THEY DON'T TELL YOU THIS

Because if they told you:

"We added 2% to your rate so we could make a few thousand dollars..."

You would say no.

So instead, they say:

"Good news—you're approved."

And then they show you:

👉 A monthly payment.

The Monthly Payment Trick (Again)

They don't emphasize:

The rate
The total interest
The spread

They emphasize:

👉 "This works for your budget."

And if it feels comfortable...

👉 Most people accept it.

Why Pre-Approval Changes Everything

This is where you take control.

Before you walk into a dealership:

👉 Go to:

A credit union
Your bank
A trusted lender

And get:

☞ A **pre-approval**

What This Gives You

Leverage.

Real leverage.

Now you walk in knowing:

Your actual rate
Your actual options
Your baseline

Now the Game Changes

If the dealership offers:

☞ A worse rate → You reject it
☞ A similar rate → You compare
☞ A better rate → You accept it

But now:

☞ You are choosing

Not guessing.

The Power Move (Advanced)

You can ask:

"What's the Buy Rate on this loan?"

Now, let's be honest:

👉 They probably won't tell you.

But the moment you ask...

👉 The dynamic changes.

Because now they know:

👉 You understand the system.

Why That Matters

When they think you don't know:

👉 They maximize the spread

When they think you *do* know:

👉 They become more careful

The Reality Most People Never See

Most people walk out of a dealership thinking:

"I got approved."

Very few walk out knowing:

"I got the best rate available."

And those are not the same thing.

Key Principle

The rate you're offered is not always the rate you earned.

Bottom Line

The Buy Rate is the real cost of money.

The Sell Rate is what you're charged.

The difference?

👉 That's where the dealership quietly makes thousands.

HOW YOU PROTECT YOURSELF

This part is simple.

Not easy.

But simple.

Rule #1 – Get Pre-Approved

Before you ever step into a dealership:

👉 Go to:

A credit union
Your bank
Any lender you trust

And get:

👉 A pre-approval

Now you walk in with:

A known interest rate
A known structure
A baseline

Why This Changes Everything

Now when the dealership offers you financing:

You can compare
You can reject it
You can negotiate

Because you're no longer blind.

Rule #2 – Ask About the Buy Rate (Optional Power Move)

You can ask:

"What's the buy rate on this loan?"

They don't have to answer.

Most won't.

But when you ask...

👉 You just changed the dynamic.

Because now they know:

👉 You know.

Rule #3 – Separate the Deal

Always remember:

Car price = one negotiation
Financing = another negotiation

Never mix them too early.

Because when they are combined...

👉 You lose visibility.

Final Truth

Financing through the dealership is not always bad.

But blind financing?

👉 That's expensive.

If you don't control your financing...

☞ Your financing will control the deal.

Bottom Line

If you don't understand how the loan works...

☞ You're not buying a car.

You're buying:

Interest
Markup
Hidden profit

One Sentence to Remember

The dealership doesn't just sell cars...
they sell money.

And sometimes...

☞ that's where they make the most.

SECTION 3 – LEASING VS. OWNERSHIP: THE PAYMENT ILLUSION

One of the slickest illusions in the car business is not the price of the car.

It is the price of the payment.

And leasing is where that illusion shines the brightest.

Because when people hear:

"You can drive this for only $399 a month"

their brain lights up.

That sounds easier.
That sounds lighter.
That sounds safer.
That sounds like a better deal.

But the monthly payment by itself does not tell you whether something is a better deal.

It only tells you whether it feels easier to swallow.

And that is a very different thing.

Why Leasing Is Usually Less Money Per Month

Leasing is almost always cheaper per month than buying the same vehicle.

That part is true.

But the reason why it is cheaper is where the illusion begins.

When you buy a car, you are paying for the full vehicle over time.

When you lease a car, you are not paying for the full vehicle.

You are basically paying for the part of the vehicle that you are expected to use during the lease term, plus fees, plus profit, plus whatever structure the lease carries.

In simple terms, the leasing company is saying:

"We know this car will still have value after three years, so you don't have to pay for the whole car. You only pay for the part you use."

That is why the monthly payment is lower.

Because you are not buying the whole thing.

You are renting its best years.

That is the payment illusion.

The monthly payment looks better not because the car became a better deal, but because you are paying for less ownership.

The Apartment Analogy

Leasing a car is a lot like renting a home.

Buying a car is a lot like buying a home.

When you buy a house, every payment you make is moving you toward ownership. Even if the beginning is heavy with interest, there is still a long-term goal: one day, it is yours.

When you rent a house or an apartment, the monthly payment may be lower than owning something comparable. It may feel simpler. It may even feel smarter in certain situations. But at the end of that rental period, you own nothing.

The same is true with a lease.

You make the payments.

You take care of the vehicle.

You drive it.

You insure it.

You maintain it.

And at the end of the term...

It is not yours.

You hand it back.

So yes, the monthly payment is lower.

But lower is not the same as better.

Lower is just lower.

What You Are Really Paying For in a Lease

When you lease a vehicle, you are typically paying for:

Depreciation during the lease term
Rent charge or finance charge
Taxes

Fees
Acquisition fee
Disposition fee in some cases
Mileage limits
Contract limitations
Penalties if applicable

So the lower payment is not some magical gift from the dealership.

It is a financial structure.

A structure designed to make the payment look attractive while keeping you inside a cycle.

Why Dealerships Love Leasing

Dealerships love leasing for several reasons.

First, the lower payment helps sell a more expensive car.

A person who would never want to buy a certain vehicle at $720 a month might lease it at $469 a month and think:

"Wow, this is much more doable."

That is exactly the point.

Leasing allows the dealership to put you into a vehicle that feels financially easier, even though the long-term value to you may be worse.

Second, leasing creates return customers.

At the end of the lease, many people do not want to:

Pay the residual and buy the car
Shop around again

Disrupt the cycle

So they just lease another one.

And another one.

And another one.

That is beautiful for the dealership.

Because now the customer is not just buying one vehicle.

👉 The customer is entering a pattern.

A pattern of permanent car payments.

The Permanent Payment Trap

This is one of the biggest problems with leasing.

You get used to the lower payment.

You get used to always driving a newer vehicle.

You get used to the idea that this is "just what you do."

And before you know it, ten years have gone by and you have made payment after payment after payment...

without owning anything.

That is where leasing can become very expensive.

Not always month to month.

But over a lifetime.

Because ownership eventually gives you breathing room.

Leasing often does not.

If you buy a car and keep it long enough, one day the payment ends.

And then you have something powerful:

A paid-off vehicle.

That changes your life more than people realize.

Because once the payment disappears, your money has somewhere else to go.

Savings.
Emergency fund.
Travel.
Investments.
A better home.
A less stressful life.

With leasing, many people never reach that stage.

They just renew the cycle.

But Is Leasing Always Bad?

No.

And this is where I want to be fair.

Leasing is not automatically stupid.

Leasing can make sense in certain situations.

For example:

You always want a newer car
You drive predictable, lower mileage
You do not want to keep vehicles long term
You want fewer repair concerns during the main term
You are okay with always having a payment
You value convenience more than ownership

If that is you, leasing may fit your lifestyle.

But that does not make it a better financial deal.

It just means it may be a better lifestyle fit.

That is an important distinction.

Some people choose leasing because they like the convenience. Fine.

Some people choose leasing because they like always driving something newer. Fine.

But many people choose leasing because the payment looks better.

That is where the illusion becomes dangerous.

Because if you are choosing based only on the monthly payment, you are not choosing wisely.

You are choosing emotionally.

The Monthly Payment Lies by Omission

A lower lease payment does not tell you:

What you will have at the end

How much total money you will spend over repeated leases
How many years you may stay in the cycle
Whether buying and keeping would have served you better

It only tells you what the present month looks like.

That is why I call it the payment illusion.

The payment is real.

But the meaning you attach to it is often false.

Ownership Has a Different Kind of Value

When you own a car, especially after the loan is paid off, the equation changes.

Now you have:

An asset you control
No mileage restrictions
No wear-and-tear penalties
No lease-end decisions forced on you
The option to keep driving without a payment

That last point matters a lot.

Because the biggest financial advantage of ownership often does not happen during the loan.

It happens after the loan.

That is when the vehicle begins to give back.

Now, of course, ownership also comes with reality:

Repairs
Maintenance
Aging vehicle issues
The possibility that at some point it becomes less convenient

That is true.

But if you buy wisely and keep the car long enough, those costs are often far less destructive than endless car payments.

Not always. But very often.

The Psychological Difference Between Leasing and Owning

There is also a mindset difference.

And this is where the home analogy matters again.

When people own something, they often relate to it differently.

There is more attachment.
More care.
More responsibility.
More long-term thinking.

When people lease or rent, the relationship is often more temporary.

Not always. But often.

And I have noticed something interesting from my own experience.

I have leased at least a dozen vehicles in my lifetime.

And every time I returned one, or even extended one, they barely looked at it.

Sometimes they did not inspect it at all.

They did not go through some dramatic, white-glove examination.

They did not kneel down with a flashlight and inspect every little detail.

In my experience, they often barely cared.

That was always surprising to me, because the way leasing is presented, you would think the return process is this strict military inspection where every tiny thing is a crisis.

But many times, that was not my experience at all.

Even when extending the contract, they often did not really inspect the vehicle.

Even when returning one to get another lease, they often did not really inspect it either.

That does not mean nobody inspects leased vehicles.

Some do.

Some situations are different.

Some damage absolutely matters.

But my experience showed me something important:

A lot of what people fear about lease returns can be exaggerated.

At the same time, that does not suddenly make leasing a better financial move.

It just means one of the fear points may not always be as severe as people imagine.

So Which One Makes You Lose More Money?

That depends on what kind of person you are.

If you buy too much car, finance too long, and trade it in constantly, buying can absolutely become expensive.

If you lease over and over again for decades and never build ownership, leasing can become very expensive too.

So the real question is not:

"Which one is always worse?"

The real question is:

"Which structure fits my long-term behavior better?"

If you are someone who keeps vehicles a long time, ownership usually wins.

If you are someone who always wants something new, does not mind endless payments, and values convenience over ownership, leasing may feel better.

But here is the problem:

Most people do not choose leasing because they consciously prefer that lifestyle.

They choose it because the payment looks easier.

That is a bad reason.

Because a lower payment can hide a weaker financial position.

The Real Test

Here is the question I would ask:

"At the end of this agreement, what do I have?"

If the answer is:

"Nothing, unless I buy it"

then you are leasing.

If the answer is:

"A vehicle that becomes mine"

then you are buying.

That one question cuts through a lot of nonsense.

When Leasing Can Make Sense

To be fair, leasing may make sense if:

You drive well within mileage limits
You truly prefer a newer vehicle every few years
You treat it more like a transportation subscription than ownership
You understand that you are paying for use, not equity
You are not fooling yourself into thinking the lower payment means better value

If you go in with open eyes, that is one thing.

If you go in hypnotized by the lower payment, that is another.

When Ownership Usually Wins

Ownership usually wins when:

You want long-term value
You plan to keep the car
You want the payment to eventually end
You want flexibility
You want to build toward no payment instead of permanent payment

That is where ownership becomes powerful.

Not flashy.

Not always easier upfront.

But powerful.

The Bottom Line

Leasing usually gives you a lower monthly payment because you are not buying the whole vehicle.

That is true.

But the lower payment is not automatically a better deal.

It may only be a prettier number.

And a prettier number is one of the oldest tricks in the car business.

Because once again, the dealership wants you looking at the payment...

instead of the long-term reality.

If you want convenience and you understand the tradeoff, leasing may fit.

If you want ownership, long-term breathing room, and a chance to eventually eliminate the payment, buying usually makes more sense.

Just do not confuse a lower monthly payment with a better financial outcome.

Those are not the same thing.

Not even close.

Final Truth

Leasing is not evil.

Ownership is not automatically superior in every single case.

But the lower lease payment is often used like bait.

And if you do not understand what that bait really means, you can spend years inside a cycle that feels affordable month to month...

while costing you far more in the long run.

SECTION 4 – THE FINAL DECISION: WHEN TO WALK VS. WHEN TO SIGN

You made it to the end.

You chose the car.
You went through the numbers.
You sat through the finance office.
You heard everything.
You saw everything.

Now comes the only moment that actually matters:

👉 The decision.

This Is the Moment Most People Get Wrong

Not because they're not smart.

Not because they didn't try.

But because they are:

Tired
Mentally drained
Emotionally invested
Ready to be done

And that combination leads to one dangerous thought:

"Let's just finish this."

That thought has cost people thousands of dollars.

The Truth About This Moment

The dealership is not rushing you.

But the situation is.

You feel the pressure—not because they're yelling...

👉 but because you want it to be over.

That's when mistakes happen.

Two Paths Exist Here

At this exact moment, there are only two real paths:

👉 **You sign**
👉 **You walk away**

There is no middle.

There is no "maybe later."

There is no "I'll fix it afterward."

Once you sign...

👉 the deal is done.

When You Should Walk Away

You should walk away if:

You don't fully understand the numbers
The OTD price is unclear

The deal changed from what you agreed on
You feel confused or rushed
The financing doesn't make sense
The numbers don't match your expectations
Something feels off

That last one matters.

👉 If something feels off... it usually is.

Walking Away Is Not Losing

Most people think walking away means:

"I failed."

That's wrong.

Walking away means:

👉 You stayed in control.

You protected your money.
You protected your decision.
You refused to commit under pressure.

That's not losing.

👉 That's discipline.

You Can Always Come Back

This is something most buyers forget:

👉 The car will still be there.

Or another one will.

There is always another car.

There is NOT always another chance to undo a bad deal.

When You Should Sign

You should sign when:

The OTD price is clear and makes sense
The numbers match what you expected
The financing is competitive or better than your pre-approval
There are no surprises
You feel calm—not rushed
You understand exactly what you are agreeing to

And most importantly:

👉 You are choosing the deal—not escaping the process

The Calm Test

Here's a simple test.

Ask yourself:

"If I walked out right now... would I regret not taking this deal?"

If the answer is:

👉 "No" → Walk away

If the answer is:

👉 "Yes, this is actually solid" → Then you're in the right place

The Silence Rule

Before you sign anything:

👉 Pause.

Take a moment.

No talking.
No pressure.
No reacting.

Just look at the numbers.

Because once you sign...

👉 everything becomes permanent.

The Emotional Trap

The dealership is counting on one thing:

👉 You being emotionally finished

Not financially satisfied.

Not logically convinced.

Just...

👉 done.

That's when people sign deals they don't fully agree with.

The Power Shift

If you made it this far and you understand everything in this book...

👉 The power is now yours.

Not theirs.

You understand:

The quadrant
The financing
The add-ons
The psychology
The timing

Now the only thing left is:

👉 execution

The Real Definition of a "Good Deal"

A good deal is not:

A low monthly payment
A fast process
A "nice" salesperson

A good deal is:

👉 One you fully understand
👉 One you are comfortable with
👉 One that aligns with your expectations

Final Truth

The dealership makes money when you sign.

You protect your money when you decide.

Bottom Line

If you feel rushed...

👉 don't sign

If you feel unsure...

👉 don't sign

If you feel pressured...

👉 don't sign

But if everything is clear...

👉 and the deal makes sense...

👉 then sign with confidence

One Sentence to Remember

You don't win at the dealership by finishing the deal...

👉 You win by making the right decision.

BONUS: BULL$HIT FEES

What They Don't Want You to Understand

There's a difference between knowing fees exist...

...and understanding how they actually work.

Most buyers reach the worksheet and think:

"Okay, these must be part of the deal."

They're not.

Not all of them.

And not in the way you think.

THE RULE THAT CHANGES EVERYTHING

There is one line you need to remember:

If it's taxable... it's negotiable.

Think about that.

Taxes are applied to:

- the selling price
- and anything treated like part of the deal

So if a fee is being taxed...

👉 it's not some fixed government charge
👉 it's part of the dealership's pricing structure

Which means:

👉 it can be reduced
👉 it can be removed
👉 it can be negotiated

That one idea alone changes how you look at the entire worksheet.

A Quick Reality Check

Not every fee will disappear.

Some dealers will push back.
Some will refuse.

But that's not the point.

👉 The point is knowing what is real... and what isn't.

Because once you know that...

👉 you stop agreeing automatically.

Where You Negotiate Matters

Most people make a critical mistake:

👉 They wait too long

They try to negotiate everything in the finance office.

That's too late.

THERE ARE TWO DIFFERENT WORLDS

Inside a dealership, there are two separate arenas:

1. The Sales Floor (Where You SHOULD Negotiate Fees)

This is where you handle:

Add-ons
Accessories
Prep charges
Packages
Anything attached to the car itself

This is your moment.

Because once you leave this phase...

👉 those items become much harder to remove

2. The Finance Office (Different Game Entirely)

This is where they sell:

Extended warranties
GAP insurance
Maintenance plans
Protection services

These are not "fees."

👉 These are **products**

And they are sold differently.

THE MISTAKE MOST BUYERS MAKE

They sit through the entire process...

Say nothing...

Then finally get to the finance office and say:

"I don't want those add-ons."

At that point?

👉 You're negotiating in the wrong room

WHY TIMING IS EVERYTHING

By the time you reach the finance office:

The deal structure is mostly set
The salesperson has already moved on
The pressure to finish is high

That's not the time to remove:

👉 accessories
👉 prep charges
👉 packages

That had to happen earlier.

USED CAR FEES: THE SNEAKY VERSION

New cars aren't the only place this happens.

Used cars come with their own version of the game.

You'll see things like:

Reconditioning fees
Inspection charges
"Vehicle prep"
Transportation

And here's the truth:

👉 All of that is already baked into the price

Why That Matters

If a dealer bought a car at auction...

👉 They already calculated:

Transportation
Repairs
Reconditioning

And they built that into the asking price.

So when they add it again as a line item?

👉 That's double charging

THE CASH TRAP

Here's another one most people never see coming.

You tell the dealer:

"I'm paying cash."

And suddenly...

👉 the deal changes

Why?

Because you just removed one of their biggest profit centers:

👉 financing

So sometimes they try to recover that profit by:

Increasing the price
Adding fees
Reducing flexibility

THE STRATEGY

Never reveal you're paying cash:

👉 until the very end

Lock the deal first.

Then decide how to pay.

ADD-ONS VS. SERVICES – KNOW THE DIFFERENCE

This is subtle, but important.

Add-Ons (Sales Floor Items)

These include:

Accessories
Cosmetic upgrades
Installed packages

☞ Negotiate these early
☞ Remove them before the deal is finalized

Services (Finance Office Products)

These include:

Warranties
Protection plans
Insurance products

☞ These are optional
☞ These are priced high
☞ These can also be negotiated

But they are a **different conversation**

THE TRUTH ABOUT VALUE

Some of these products are not completely useless.

But here's the problem:

☞ They are almost always overpriced

So even if you want something...

☞ You should never pay full price

THE PATTERN YOU NEED TO SEE

Across all these fees, there is a pattern:

They sound official
They appear late in the process
They rely on your fatigue
They assume you won't push back

And most importantly:

👉 They are rarely questioned

Final Truth

Dealerships don't expect you to understand every fee.

They expect you to accept them.

Bottom Line

You don't beat BS fees by arguing.

👉 You beat them by understanding:

What they are
When they appear
Where to negotiate them

One Sentence to Remember

If you don't question the fees...

☞ you will pay them.

Now Let's Make This Real

Everything you just learned is theory.

Now let's look at what this actually looks like...

☞ on real dealership worksheets
☞ with real numbers
☞ from real deals

Because once you see it...

☞ you can't unsee it.

STOP LETTING DEALERS ROB YOU WITH BS FEES (WHAT THIS LOOKS LIKE IN THE REAL WORLD)

The Hidden Charges That Quietly Inflate Your Deal

There's a moment in every car deal where everything looks fine.

The price seems reasonable.
The monthly payment feels okay.
The salesperson is smiling.

And then...

👉 the worksheet shows up.

And suddenly, your deal is full of:

Fees
Add-ons
Packages
Charges you never asked for

And most people do one of two things:

👉 Ignore them
👉 Or assume they're required

That's where the money disappears.

The Truth About "Fees"

Let's get something straight:

Not all fees are real.

Some are legitimate:

Taxes
Registration
Title fees

But many others?

- Pure profit
- Completely negotiable
- Or completely made up

The Illusion of Legitimacy

They don't call them:

"Extra profit charges"

They call them:

Protection packages
Prep fees
Documentation
Environmental
Security systems

They are designed to:

- sound official
- look required
- feel non-negotiable

But they are not.

The Most Common BS Charges

Let's break down what's really happening.

Freight → Already included in MSRP
Dealer Prep → Already reimbursed by manufacturer
Doc Fee → Often inflated and non-negotiable (but still profit-driven)
Unknown Fees (like PIPA) → Undefined, unjustified, and questionable

👉 These are not value-based charges
👉 These are margin tools

Why Dealers Add These

Simple:

👉 Because most people don't question them

And remember:

If you don't ask... you don't get

That applies to BOTH sides.

REAL EXAMPLES OF BS FEES (FROM ACTUAL DEALS)

These are not made up.

These are real fees, from real dealership worksheets, with real prices.

Example 1 – Dealer Worksheet Breakdown

Freight: **$2,097.00**

Doc Fee: **$150.00**
Dealer Prep: **$1,688.00**
PIPA (unknown charge): **$349.00**

These alone add over **$4,000+** to the deal

Example 2 – "Protection & Add-On Packages"

Alloy Cosmetic Wheel Protection: **$599.00**
3-Year Paintless Dent Repair: **$795.00**
Decor Package: **$895.00**
Nitro Filled Tires: **$595.00**
Enviro Seal: **$610.00**

Total: Over **$3,400** in add-ons most people never asked for

Example 3 – Add-On Line Items

Nitro: **$199.99**
Capital 3M Protection: **$595.99**
Triton Car Care System: **$398.00**
Spray-in Bedliner: **$899.99**

These are often bundled and quietly added

Example 4 – Common "Accessory" Add-Ons

(No prices shown—but these are commonly charged extras)

Splash Guards
Mud Guards
Exhaust Tip
Pinstripes
Sun Shade
Floor Mats

Connectivity Kit
Trunk Tray
Pro Pack

👉 These are often pre-installed and priced later

Example 5 – Protection & "Security" Products

KARR Security System
Fusion Security System
Theft Prevent
Data Dots / Nano Dots
US TheftGuard

👉 These sound critical
👉 But are often overpriced and unnecessary

Example 6 – Cosmetic & Protection Upsells

Nitrogen Fill
Solar Guard Tint
Nano-Ceramic Film
Smart Auto Windshield
Windshield Repair Packages
Crystal Fusion
Diamond Coat
Paint & Interior Protection

👉 High margin
👉 Low necessity

What You Must Understand

These fees exist for one reason:

👉 To increase profit without increasing the car price

Because if they raise the car price directly:

👉 You notice

But if they spread it across "fees":

👉 You accept it

THE STRATEGY TO BEAT THIS

It's simple.

Not easy.

But simple.

Step 1 – Always Ask for the OTD Breakdown

You want to see:

👉 Every line item

Step 2 – Question Everything

If you don't recognize it:

👉 Ask

If it sounds vague:

👉 Challenge it

Step 3 – Remove What You Didn't Ask For

Say:

"I don't want this. Remove it."

Not:

"Can you remove it?"

Step 4 – Be Willing to Walk

Because sometimes they'll say:

"We can't remove that."

And your answer is:

👉 "Then I can't buy this."

THE EMOTIONAL TRICK

These fees are usually presented:

At the end
After hours of discussion
When you're tired

That's not an accident.

That's timing.

Final Truth

You don't get charged these fees because they are required.

☞ You get charged them because you didn't stop them.

Bottom Line

Every fee you don't understand...

☞ is a fee you shouldn't accept

One Sentence to Remember

If it's not required by law...

☞ It's negotiable—or removable.

Most people don't overpay because they're stupid or careless...

☞ They overpay because they didn't know what to question.

BONUS: THE $4 A DAY LIE: HOW THE FINANCE OFFICE SELLS YOU $9,300 WITHOUT YOU NOTICING

The Finance Office Is Not Paperwork… It's a Second Sale

You negotiated the price.
You shook hands.
You think you won.

Then they walk you into another room.

Different person.
Different tone.
Different strategy.

This is not paperwork.

This is **round two**.

THE SETUP: "PROTECTING YOUR INVESTMENT"

They won't say:

"We're about to sell you $7,500 worth of high-margin products."

Instead, you'll hear:

"Let's go over some options to protect your investment."

Sounds responsible.

Sounds smart.

It's neither.

It's a sales presentation.

The Three-Tier Trap

You're not presented with one option.

You're presented with three:

Gold
Platinum
Diamond

And this is not random.

This is engineered.

Because once you're choosing between options...
you've already stopped asking the most important question:

👉 *"Do I need any of this at all?"*

WHAT THEY SHOW YOU

On the screen or printed sheet, it looks clean, simple, and logical.

At the top, your base payment is shown.
In this example:

👉 **$603/month**

Then come the three tiers.

🟡 Gold Plan

Extended Warranty: **YES**
Everything else: **NO**

That's it.

No paint protection.
No tire coverage.
No GAP insurance.
No interior protection.
No key replacement.

👉 Monthly impact: +**$49/month**
👉 New payment: **$652/month**

This is your **entry point**.

It exists for one reason:

👉 To make the next option look better.

🔘 Platinum Plan

Now things start stacking.

Extended Warranty: **YES**
Paint & Exterior Protection: **YES**
Tire & Wheel Coverage: **YES**
Everything else: **NO**

Now you're thinking:

"Okay... this actually makes more sense."

That's intentional.

👉 Monthly impact: +**$95/month**
👉 New payment: **$698/month**

This is the **middle anchor**.

It feels "balanced."

But it's not the target.

🔘 Diamond Plan (The Real Target)

Now everything is included:

Extended Warranty: **YES**
Paint & Exterior Protection: **YES**
Tire & Wheel Coverage: **YES**
GAP Insurance: **YES**
Interior Fabric Protection: **YES**
Key Replacement Program: **YES**

Everything.

Nothing left out.

No risk.

No regret.

That's the emotional hook.

👉 Monthly impact: +**$129/month**
👉 New payment: **$732/month**

And right underneath it, you'll almost always see:

"Most customers choose Diamond."

What Just Happened?

Let's slow that down.

You walked in thinking:

👉 "I'm buying a car for $603/month."

Now you're looking at:

👉 $652 → $698 → $732

And your brain says:

"Well... if I'm already here... what's another $30?"

That's the trap.

The Design Behind It

This is not a menu.

This is psychology.

Gold feels too basic
Platinum feels reasonable
Diamond feels safe

And humans don't like feeling:

cheap
exposed
or regretful

So they move up.

The Real Question You Should Be Asking

Not:

"Which one should I choose?"

But:

"Why am I choosing any of these?"

Because once you say:

👉 "I'll take Diamond"

You didn't just add $129/month.

You just added:

👉 **~$9,000+ to your loan**

Final Truth

They didn't sell you three options.

They guided you to one.

And they did it without ever forcing you.

That's why it works.

Gold is the decoy. Platinum is the bridge. **Diamond is the sale.**

THE PSYCHOLOGICAL PUSH

You'll hear something like:

"Most customers choose the Diamond package."

Of course they do.

Because:

It sounds like the "smart" choice
It feels like the "complete" choice
It avoids regret

But here's the reality:

They are not selling you protection.

They are selling you **comfort disguised as logic**.

The $4 a Day Illusion

This is where it gets dangerous.

Instead of saying:

"This package costs $7,393..."

They say:

"It's only $4 a day."

Let that sink in.

Because your brain does this:

$4 → small
daily → harmless
coffee comparison → relatable

So you relax.

But the math tells a different story.

The Real Numbers (What They Don't Want You to See)

From the actual breakdown:

Extended Warranty: **$2,800**
Paint Protection: **$1,200**
Tire & Wheel: **$1,400**
GAP Insurance: **~$895**
Interior Protection: **$599**
Key Replacement: **$499**

👉 Total: **~$7,393**

Now add financing over **72 months**

👉 Real total: **~$9,300+**

That "$4 a day" just became:

👉 **Almost ten thousand dollars**

The Profit Reality

Here's the part nobody tells you:

Dealer cost: **~$1,625**
You pay: **~$7,393**

👉 Dealer profit: **~$5,768**

👉 Profit margin: **~78%**

This is not a side sale.

This is the business.

GAP INSURANCE (THE ONLY ONE THAT MIGHT MATTER)

Let's be fair.

Not everything here is useless.

GAP insurance can actually make sense.

Here's why:
You owe: $30,000

Car value after accident: $20,000
Insurance pays: $20,000

👉 You still owe: **$10,000**

That's the "gap."

GAP insurance covers that.

But here's the catch:

It's often overpriced at dealerships
You can get it cheaper through:
your insurance company
your bank or credit union

So even the "useful" product...

👉 is still being sold the wrong way

The Real Trick: Hiding the Price

The biggest red flag is not the product.

It's this moment:

You ask:

"How much is each item?"

And they respond with:

"It's only $4 a day."

That's not an answer.

That's a deflection.

The Right Move (What You Should Do)

When you're in that chair, do this:

1. ASK FOR ITEMIZED PRICING

Not monthly.
Not daily.

👉 Full price.

2. SEPARATE EVERYTHING

You are not buying a "package."

You are evaluating:

warranty
GAP
tire coverage
etc.

Individually.

3. NEGOTIATE (YES, YOU CAN)

This is the part most people don't know:

👉 Every single one of these is negotiable

4. CROSS-SHOP

You can:

call another dealership
check online
ask your insurance

Yes... even after you bought the car.

5. BE READY TO SAY NO

The most powerful sentence in the finance office:

"I decline all coverages."

Final Thought

The dealership doesn't celebrate when you buy the car.

They celebrate when you say yes in this room.

Because this is where:

emotion beats logic
small numbers hide big ones
and "peace of mind" becomes profit

Once you understand this...

You don't get sold.

You decide.

BONUS: QUICK-REFERENCE CHEAT SHEET

🚗 Car Buying Glossary 🚘

This is your **quick-reference cheat sheet**—a simplified breakdown of the most important terms, numbers, and concepts in this book.

This page is your **dealership survival sheet**.

Use it as your **on-the-spot guide** when you're inside a dealership.

👉 Keep it on your phone.
👉 Screenshot it.
👉 Print it.
👉 Bring it with you.

If you'd like a printable PDF version, visit:
www.benjamintemplar.com

CAR BUYING GLOSSARY

QUICK-REFERENCE CHEAT SHEET

HOW TO BUY A CAR AT HE DEALERSHIP AND NOT GET RIPPED OFF THAT BADLY — WRITTEN BY BENJAMIN A. TEMPLAR

REMEMBER:
FOCUS ON THE OUT-THE-DOOR (OTD) PRICE.
NOT THE MONTHLY PAYMENT.

MSRP
(Manufacturer's Suggested Retail Price)
The official price the manufacturer recommends the dealership sell the vehicle for. It is often referred to as the "sticker price" and is typically higher than what the dealer actually pays for the vehicle.

INVOICE PRICE
The amount the dealership is billed by the manufacturer for the vehicle. It does not include additional hidden incentives and payments the dealer receives.

OTD (OUT-THE-DOOR PRICE)
The total, final cost of the vehicle, including the selling price, taxes, fees, add-ons, and everything required to complete the purchase.
This is the only number that matters.

TRADE-IN VALUE
The amount the dealership offers you for your current vehicle. It is a negotiation tool and can be manipulated, so research its real market value first.

DOC FEE
(DOCUMENTATION FEE)
A charge by the dealership to cover paperwork and administrative costs. Often inflated and is dealer profit disguised as a fee.

DELIVERY, PROCESSING & HANDLING (DPH)
A fee charged by the manufacturer to cover transporting, handling, and delivering the vehicle to the dealership. Not the same as the doc fee. It is non-negotiable.

DOWN PAYMENT
The amount of money paid upfront when purchasing a vehicle. It reduces the total loan amount, lowers monthly payments, and can reduce total interest paid.

CREDIT SCORE
A numerical rating (typically 300–850) that represents your creditworthiness. It directly impacts loan approval, interest rates, and financing terms.

MONTHLY PAYMENT
The amount paid each month toward a vehicle loan. Includes principal, interest, and sometimes taxes, fees, and add-ons. Focusing only on this number can hide the true total cost.

BUMPER-TO-BUMPER WARRANTY
Covers most components of the car from front to back, excluding normal wear-and-tear items. Typically limited by time or mileage (e.g., 3 years/36,000 miles).

DAY SUPPLY (DAYS' SUPPLY OF INVENTORY)
How long a dealership's current inventory will last based on the current sales pace. Higher day supply = more negotiating power for you.

BUY RATE
The lowest interest rate a lender approves for you based on your credit profile. Dealers may mark up this rate for profit.

SELL RATE
The interest rate the dealership presents to you. It is often higher than the buy rate; the difference is kept by the dealer as profit.

ALLOCATION SWAP
A dealer trade that allows one dealership to receive a vehicle instead of the original dealership it was assigned to.

BELOW-THE-LINE MONEY
Manufacturer payments to the dealer that are not visible to you and are not included in the invoice. These increase the dealer's real profit.

ADVERTISING ASSISTANCE – Manufacturer money to help cover marketing/advertising costs (e.g., ~$400 on a $40,000 car).

FLOOR PLAN ASSISTANCE – Manufacturer money to help dealers offset the cost of financing inventory (e.g., ~$800).

HOLDBACK – 1.5% to 3% of the base MSRP paid back to the dealer by the manufacturer after the vehicle sells (usually quarterly) (e.g., ~$800 on a $40,000 car).

TRUE DEALER COST (REAL COST) – The actual cost to the dealer after all manufacturer incentives. Usually lower than invoice.

TOTAL DEALER PROFIT – The full profit the dealer makes: visible margin (invoice to MSRP) + hidden incentives. Often double what buyers think.

PROTECTION & ADD-ONS

EXTENDED WARRANTY (VEHICLE SERVICE CONTRACT)
A paid plan that extends coverage beyond the factory warranty. Usually marked up significantly.

GAP INSURANCE
Covers the difference between what you owe on your loan and the vehicle's actual value if it's totaled or stolen.

ADD-ONS
Dealer-installed or optional products like paint protection, window tint, theft protection, VIN etching, tracking devices, etc. Often overpriced and negotiable.

DANGER TERMS

MONTHLY PAYMENT
Easy to manipulate.

SELL RATE
Often marked up for profit.

ADD-ONS
High profit, low value.

MARKET ADJUSTMENT
Extra charge based on supply & demand.

PAYMENT PACKING
Extra products hidden inside your payment.

KEY PRINCIPLE

It doesn't matter where the money is labeled—only how much you're paying in total.

**FOCUS ON THE OTD PRICE.
NEGOTIATE THE TOTAL DEAL.
NOT JUST ONE NUMBER.**

SMART BUYER REMINDERS

- ✓ Get pre-approved with your bank or credit union.
- ✓ Know your trade-in value before you walk in.
- ✓ Always ask for the OTD price in writing.
- ✓ Negotiate the price of the car first, then the trade-in.
- ✓ Question every fee and every add-on.
- ✓ You can always walk away.

OTD FORMULA

SELLING PRICE
– REBATES / INCENTIVES
+ DOC FEE
+ GOVERNMENT FEES
+ SALES TAX
+ ADD-ONS (IF ANY)
= OUT-THE-DOOR PRICE

FINAL WORD

The more you understand, the more power you have.
**Knowledge is your best negotiating tool.
Use it.**

BONUS: STRAWS® COMIC

The Dealership in Real Life: What They Don't Say Out Loud

Before this book became what it is today—structured, tactical, and built to give you control inside a dealership—there was something much simpler.

A pen.
A piece of paper.
And a few straws.

Back in the first edition of this book (around 2008), I created a series of comic strips called **"Straws."**

They were simple.
Minimal.
Almost childish in appearance.

But the ideas behind them?

👉 Not childish at all.

WHAT ARE THE "STRAWS"?

The Straws are exactly what they look like:

👉 Characters made out of... straws.

No fancy design.
No complex anatomy.
Just simple shapes—lines, circles, and expressions.

And yet...

👉 They tell very real stories.

Stories about:

Sales tactics
Pressure
Confusion
Psychological tricks
And the quiet moments where buyers lose control of the deal

The Salesperson

You'll notice one character stands out.

The salesperson.

He's easy to recognize:

👉 The big hairdo.
👉 The confident posture.
👉 The constant smile.

That exaggerated hairstyle wasn't random.

It was intentional.

👉 A visual signal.

A way to instantly distinguish the one person in the scene who is:

👉 **Running the game.**

Then vs. Now

What you're about to see are the **original Straws comics** from the first edition.

The dialogue?

👉 **Exactly the same.**

Word for word.

Nothing rewritten.
Nothing softened.
Nothing modernized.

Because the truth is...

👉 These conversations haven't changed.

The Only Difference

The visuals.

Back then, these comics were hand-drawn—raw, imperfect, and unpolished.

In this edition:

👉 They've been enhanced and refined using modern tools and AI.

Cleaner lines.
Better structure.
Sharper presentation.

But the soul of them?

👉 Untouched.

Why They Matter

These comics are not just for entertainment.

They are:

👉 **Snapshots of reality.**

Exaggerated?
Sometimes.

Accurate?
More often than most people are comfortable admitting.

Each strip represents a moment you might experience:

A question that sounds innocent... but isn't
An offer that sounds generous... but isn't
A decision that feels right... but isn't

How to Read Them

Don't just read them.

👉 Study them.

Ask yourself:

What is really happening here?
Who is controlling the conversation?
Where does the buyer lose leverage?

Because once you see the pattern...

👉 You'll start recognizing it in real life.

Final Thought

These Straws may look simple.

But the game they expose?

👉 Isn't.

Enjoy them.

And more importantly...

👉 Learn from them.

Comic # 1

Straws©
Car Dealership Edition
by Benjamin A. Templar
T
S
WHAT'S THAT TAKARU'S PRICE?
THAT SUKURU'S PRICE IS ONLY $199* A MONTH
NO, I MEAN **THAT** TAKARU'S PRICE
THAT SUKURU'S PRICE IS ONLY $199* A MONTH
I AM NOT INTERESTED ON **THAT** CAR. I ONLY WANT TO KNOW THAT TAKARU'S PRICE
THAT SUKURU'S PRICE IS ONLY $199* A MONTH
FINE, NEVER MIND...
SIGN WHERE THE 'X' IS PLEASE
SUKURU
X

Comic # 2

STRAWS©
CAR DEALERSHIP EDITION
BY BENJAMIN A. TEMPLAR
HI...
HELLO, CAN I GET YOUR SSN AND YOUR SIGNATURE HERE PLEASE?
BUT...
SIGN HERE DAMN IT AND YOUR SSN OVER HERE PLEASE
BLA
BLA~
X
...
OFFICE
BAD CREDIT
BAD CREDIT
SECURITY! PLEASE REMOVE THIS SCUMBAG STRANGER FROM THE MAIN LOT ASAP!

Comic # 3

"Straws©" Car Dealership Edition
by Benjamin A. Templar
Hi...
HELLO, CAN I GET YOUR SSN AND YOUR SIGNATURE HERE PLEASE ?
BUT...
SIGN HERE DAMN IT AND YOUR SSN OVER HERE PLEASE
OFFICE
• • •
GOOD CREDIT
WELCOME MR. SMITH! WOULD YOU LIKE SOME CAVIAR, CHAMPAGNE, AND A CIGAR?

Comic # 4

Straws© Car Dealership Edition
by Benjamin A. Templar
WHICH CAR WOULD YOU LIKE?
I WANT THAT BRAND NEW SPECIAL EDITION OVER THERE...
HOW MUCH CAN YOU AFFORD ON A CAR PAYMENT?
ABOUT A HUNDRED AND FIFTY...
OK... I'LL BE RIGHT BACK!
3 MINUTES LATER
SIGN HERE PLEASE
I MR. SMITH, agree
of $150
for 720 MONTHS.
X

Comic # 5

Straws©
Car Dealership EDITION
by Benjamin A. Templar
IS THAT THE CAR YOU NEED?
NO, IT'S NOT
YES, THAT IS THE CAR YOU NEED
?
CAN YOU PAY $900 A MONTH FOR IT?
NO, I CAN'T...
YES YOU CAN SIGN HERE PLEASE
?
SIGN HERE
$900 x 72

Comic # 6

Straws©
Car Dealership Edition
by Benjamin A. Templar
WHAT DO YOU DO FOR A LIVING MR. SMITH?
I AM A NURSE.
MY BEST FRIEND IS A NURSE TOO. DO YOU LIKE ME MORE NOW?
NO, I DON'T.
DO YOU LIVE AROUND HERE?
I LIVE IN BROWNSVILLE VERMONT.
MY MOM LIVES THERE TOO. DO YOU LIKE ME NOW?
NO, I WON'T BUY A CAR FROM YOU.

Comic # 7

Straws© Car Dealership Edition
by Benjamin A. Templar
AND THIS IS CALLED 'MARBLES INSURANCE' AND YOU CAN GET IT FOR ONLY $1 A DAY. WHAT CAN YOU BUY WITH A DOLLAR A DAY? A CAN OF SODA. YOU CUT A CAN OF SODA A DAY AND YOU LOOSE 30 POUNDS A YEAR.
WHAT'S 'MARBLES INSURANCE'?
IT'S AN INSURANCE THAT COVERS YOU ONLY IN CASE ON A SUNDAY AFTERNOON YOUR CHILDREN ARE PLAYING WITH MARBLES AND YOU HAPPEND TO WALK AROUND, STEP ON THEM BY ACCIDENT, FALL AND BRAKE ANY OF BOTH ARMS OR ANY OF BOTH LEGS AND BECHIUSE...
NO, THANKS
LOOK, I DON'T MEAN TO SCARE YOU... BUT MY CHILDREN AND I PLAY A LOT OF MARBLES TOGETHER AND I FELL ONCE AND ALMOST BROKE MY RIGHT LEG...
?

Comic # 8

Straws© Car Dealership Edition
by Benjamin A. Templar
MY BOSS IS IN A GREAT MOOD TODAY AND- TOLD ME HE WILL GIVE YOU $5,000 ON TRADE-IN VALUE FOR YOUR VEHICLE
WHAT?! I PAID $20,000 LAST YEAR WHEN I BOUGHT IT BRAND NEW!
WELL BUT, TO TELL YOU THE TRUTH, NEW CARS DEPRECIATE A LOT ON VALUE AS SOON AS YOU DRIVE THEM OUT OF THE DEALERSHIP AND HE WAS GOING TO GIVE YOU $4,000 BUT HE WANTS TO SELL A LOT OF CARS TODAY... WANNA DO IT?
Ok...
GOOD!

Comic # 9

Straws©
Car Dealership EDITION
by Benjamin A. Templar
When good credit...
KNOW WHAT CAR YOU NEED?
WHAT CAR DO I NEED?
THE CAR I NEED TO SELL
WHAT CAR DO YOU NEED TO SELL ME?
THE MOST EXPENSIVE ONE YOU CAN AFFORD
OR NOT

Comic # 10

STRAWS© CAR DEALERSHIP EDITION
BY BENJAMIN A. TEMPLAR
IF YOU PROMISE ME YOU'LL BUY A NEW CAR TODAY I'LL GIVE YOU A FREE KEYCHAIN
IT'S THE KEYCHAIN BRAND NEW?
IT'S BRAND NEW AND CUTE. WANNA DO IT?
OK, I PROMISE!

Comic # 11

Straws©
Car Dealership EDITION
by Benjamin A. Templar
WANNA DO IT ON 60 PAYMENTS OF $480 OR 72 PAYMENTS OF $479?
WHAT'S THE DIFFERENCE?
WITH 72 MONTHS YOU HAVE MORE TIME TO PAY AND IT IS CHEAPER
OH, WELL... 72 I GUESS...
OK, SIGN HERE PLEASE
HA HA!
72
479

Comic # 12

STRAWS© CAR DEALERSHIP EDITION
by Benjamin A. Templar
I NEED A TRUCK.
NO, YOU DON'T. YOU NEED THAT SUV.
4WD TRUCK THEN...
YOU NEED THAT SUV.
FINE. I'LL TAKE IT.
GOOD CHOICE. SIGN HERE.
CONTRACT

Comic # 13

Straws© Car Dealership Edition
by Benjamin A. Templar
HELLO MR..?
MR. SMITH
MR. SMITH, WOULD YOU LIKE TO TEST DRIVE THAT VEHICLE?
NO THANKS. I AM NOT INTERSTED IN THAT VEHICLE AT ALL,
?
OK, I'LL BE RIGHT BACK WITH THE KEYS THEN...!

Comic # 14

STRAWS©
CAR DEALERSHIP EDITION
by Benjamin A. Templar
YOU ARE GOING TO BUY WHATEVER I WANT YOU TO BUY, YOU HEAR ME?!
NO, I WON'T BECAUSE I AM THE CUSTOMER AND THE CUSTOMER IS ALWAYS RIGHT...
IF YOU ARE THE CUSTOMER AND YOU ARE ALWAYS RIGHT, I AM THE CAR SALESMAN AND I AM ALWAYS WRONG THAT MEANS YOU ARE GOING TO BUY WHATEVER YOU WANT THEN.
OK, I AM GOING TO BUY WHATEVER YOU WANT ME TO. WHERE SHOULD I SIGN?
SIGN HERE PLEASE
WHAT EVER

Comic # 15

Straws©
Car Dealership EDITION
by Benjamin A. Templar
HI, I CAME TO RETRIEVE MY $10,000 CHRISTMAS SPECIAL DISCOUNT COUPON WHEN YOU BUY A NEW CAR!
DID YOU READ THE SMALL LETTERS?
NO...
IT SAYS: "ONLY WHITH THE PURCHASE OF A $75,000+, 15 MPG OR LESS HUGE OVER PRICED TRUCK. VALID UNTIL CHRISTMAS DAY."
DO YOU WANT YOUR $10,000 DISCOUNT THEN?
SURE, BUT... DO I STILL HAVE TIME?
NOT MUCH, BUT STILL SOME. LET ME PICK ONE FOR YOU SON. SIGN HERE PLEASE
HO HO HO!
OVER PRICED TRUCK

GLOSSARY

Car Dealership Language (Jargon)

MSRP (Manufacturer's Suggested Retail Price)

The **official** price the manufacturer recommends the dealership sell the vehicle for. It is often referred to as the "sticker price" and is typically higher than what the dealer actually pays for the vehicle. It is the price you see on the window sticker of a new car.
👉 **"Sticker Price"**

What MSRP Represents

The MSRP is the manufacturer's *recommended* selling price for a vehicle based on:

Base model cost
Trim level
Factory-installed options
Destination (shipping) charges

It is meant to create a **standardized starting point** for pricing across all dealerships.

What MSRP Is NOT

This is where most buyers get confused.

👉 MSRP is **not**:

The final price you will pay
The Out-the-Door (OTD) price

A guaranteed price
A fixed or non-negotiable number

It is simply a **suggestion**.

The keyword is:

Suggested

Why MSRP Exists

Manufacturers use MSRP to:

Maintain pricing consistency across dealerships
Position the vehicle in the market
Give buyers a reference point

But dealerships are independent businesses.

They are not required to sell at MSRP.

What Actually Happens in the Real World

The selling price of a vehicle can be:

Below MSRP (discounted)
At MSRP (standard pricing)
Above MSRP (market adjustment)

This depends on:

Supply and demand
Popularity of the vehicle
Market conditions
Dealer strategy

The Hidden Strategy Around MSRP

MSRP is often used as a **psychological anchor**.

For example:

MSRP: $50,000
Dealer price: $47,500

This makes it feel like:

👉 "You're saving $2,500"

Even if the real market value of the car is closer to $47,000 or less.

The Rebate Confusion

Another common trick involves **manufacturer rebates**.

Example:

MSRP: $50,000
Rebate: $2,500

The dealership may present this as:

👉 "We're giving you a $2,500 discount"

But in reality:

👉 The manufacturer—not the dealer—is providing that rebate.

So the true negotiation should still happen **before the rebate is applied**.

MSRP vs. OTD (Critical Difference)

This is one of the most important distinctions in the entire car-buying process:

MSRP = Starting point
OTD Price = Final reality

MSRP does NOT include:

Taxes
Dealer fees
Registration
Add-ons
Financing costs

OTD includes all of it.

What You Should Do With MSRP

Use MSRP as:

👉 A reference point—not a decision point

Your goal is to:

Compare MSRP across multiple dealerships
Identify consistency in pricing
Negotiate the selling price **below MSRP when possible**
Then calculate the **OTD price**

Key Principle

MSRP is where the conversation begins—
not where the deal is made.

Bottom Line

The MSRP is the manufacturer's suggested price, not the real price.

It is useful for comparison, but it does not reflect:

- What you will actually pay
- Or whether you are getting a good deal

If you focus on MSRP, you are looking at the surface.

If you focus on OTD...

- You are seeing the truth.

Invoice Price

The amount the dealership is billed by the manufacturer for the vehicle. It is commonly believed to represent the dealer's true cost, but in reality, it does **not include additional hidden incentives and payments** the dealer receives from the manufacturer.

OTD (Out-the-Door Price)

The **Out-the-Door Price (OTD)** is the **total, final cost of a vehicle**, including *everything* required to complete the purchase.

It represents the **entire transaction rolled into one number**—the amount you would pay if you walked in with a check and bought the car outright on the spot.

What OTD Includes

The OTD price is not just the price of the car. It is a combination of multiple components, typically including:

Selling Price – The negotiated price of the vehicle
Rebates/Incentives – Discounts from the manufacturer (subtracted from the price)
Dealer Fees (Doc Fee) – Administrative or processing fees charged by the dealership
Government Fees – Title, registration, and licensing costs
Sales Tax – Based on your state and local regulations
Add-ons (if applicable) – Optional or dealer-installed items such as:
Paint protection
Theft protection
Accessories
Tracking systems (e.g., LoJack)

Example Breakdown

Using a real-world example:

Selling Price: **$57,632**
Rebate: **−$2,500**
Adjusted Price: **$55,132**

Then adding:

Doc Fee: **$799**
Government Fees: **$355**
Sales Tax: **$2,449.36**

Final OTD Price: $58,735.36

This is the number that matters—not the monthly payment, not the sticker price, not any single line item.

👉 **This is the real cost of the car.**

Why OTD Is So Important

The OTD price eliminates confusion.

Instead of juggling multiple numbers, you reduce the entire deal to one simple question:

"How much am I paying in total?"

This prevents the dealership from:

Hiding fees
Shifting numbers between categories
Distracting you with monthly payments
Creating the illusion of a "better deal"

Common Mistakes Buyers Make

Many buyers focus on the wrong numbers:

Monthly payment
Sticker price (MSRP)
Trade-in value alone

These numbers can all be manipulated.

The OTD price cannot.

What to Watch Out For

Some dealerships may:

Add hidden or vague fees
Bundle unnecessary add-ons

Avoid clearly presenting the full breakdown

Always request a **complete itemized breakdown** of the OTD price so you can see:

👉 What you are paying
👉 And why you are paying it

Key Principle

If you don't know the Out-the-Door price, you don't know the deal.

Bottom Line

The OTD price is the **only number that truly matters in a car purchase**.

Everything else is part of the structure.

👉 The OTD is the reality.

Trade-In Value

The **Trade-In Value** is the amount of money a dealership offers you for your current vehicle when you apply it toward the purchase of another car.

Instead of selling your car privately, you "trade it in," and the dealership subtracts that value from the overall deal.

What Trade-In Value Represents

In theory, the trade-in value reflects:

The condition of your vehicle
Mileage
Age
Market demand
Comparable sales

In practice...

👉 It is also a **negotiation tool**.

Why Trade-In Value Is Tricky

Most buyers think:

"If I get a higher trade-in value, I'm getting a better deal."

Not necessarily.

Because the dealership is not negotiating one number.

👉 They are negotiating multiple numbers at the same time.

So they can:

Increase your trade-in value
While increasing the price of the new car
Or adjusting your down payment
Or shifting the structure of the deal

And it can *look* like they helped you...

👉 When they didn't.

The Illusion of a "Great Trade-In Offer"

You might hear something like:

"Good news—we were able to give you $1,000 more for your trade."

That sounds like a win.

But if they quietly added $1,500 to the price of the new vehicle...

👉 You actually lost money.

What Your Trade-In Is REALLY Worth

The real value of your vehicle is not determined by one dealership.

It is determined by the **market**.

That's why it's critical to check your value before walking in.

How to Estimate Your Trade-In Value

Before going to a dealership, you should get at least **2–3 independent estimates** from sources such as:

Kelley Blue Book (KBB)
Carvana
Other online appraisal tools

Enter:

Your VIN
Mileage
Condition
Features

This gives you:

👉 A **realistic value range**

Not an exact number—but a range you can trust.

Why This Matters

If your research shows:

$14,500
$15,200

Then you know your car is worth roughly:

👉 $14K–$15K

Now when a dealership offers:

👉 $12,000

You don't guess.

You don't wonder.

👉 You know it's low.

The "We Need to See the Car" Line

You will often hear:

"We can't give you a trade-in value without seeing the car."

Sometimes that's valid.

But in many cases...

👉 It's just a way to get you into the dealership.

Because once you're there:

You're invested
You're more likely to proceed
The negotiation becomes harder to control

And here's the reality:

Many dealerships don't do a deep inspection.

They may:

Look at the car briefly
Walk around it
Or sometimes barely inspect it at all

Which tells you something important:

👉 They often already have a number in mind.

Trade-In vs. Selling Privately

Trading in is convenient.

Fast
Simple
No hassle

But it often comes at a cost.

Selling privately can:

Take more time
Require more effort

But may get you:

👉 More money

So the real question is:

Do you value convenience... or maximum value?

When to Discuss Trade-In

This is critical.

👉 Do NOT discuss your trade-in too early.

Always:

Lock the **Out-the-Door (OTD) price** first
Then negotiate the trade-in separately

Why?

Because combining both too early allows the dealership to:

👉 Hide profit inside the structure of the deal

Key Principle

A higher trade-in value does NOT mean a better deal.

Only the **combined outcome** matters.

Bottom Line

The trade-in value is just one part of a larger equation.

On its own, it can be manipulated.

👉 Only when separated from the rest of the deal...
👉 and compared to real market data...

...does it become meaningful.

Doc Fee (Documentation Fee)

The **Doc Fee**—short for **Documentation Fee**—is a charge added by the dealership to cover the cost of processing paperwork for your vehicle purchase.

This may include:

Preparing contracts
Filing title and registration documents
Handling administrative tasks
Submitting forms to the state

What It Sounds Like

It sounds official.

It sounds necessary.

It sounds like:

"This is just part of buying a car."

What It Actually Is

👉 The Doc Fee is **dealer profit disguised as an administrative cost**.

Yes, paperwork exists.

Yes, someone processes it.

But the reality is:

👉 The actual cost of processing paperwork is relatively small.

The Doc Fee is often:

👉 Inflated well beyond the real cost.

Typical Doc Fee Ranges

Doc fees vary widely depending on the state and dealership:

Some states cap the fee (e.g., \$75–\$200)
Other states allow it to go much higher
Many dealerships charge **\$500–\$1,000+**

And here's the key:

👉 The higher the fee, the more profit is built into it.

Why Dealerships Use Doc Fees

Because it allows them to:

Advertise a lower vehicle price
Add profit later in the deal
Make the fee seem "non-negotiable"

You might hear:

"This fee is required."
"Everyone pays this."
"It's standard."

And while it may be standard...

👉 That doesn't mean it's fair.

The Non-Negotiable Illusion

Many dealerships claim the Doc Fee is:

👉 "Non-negotiable"

Technically, the fee itself might not be removed.

But that doesn't mean you can't negotiate around it.

How Smart Buyers Handle Doc Fees

You don't argue about the fee itself.

👉 You adjust the deal around it.

For example:

If the Doc Fee is $800
You negotiate $800 off the vehicle price

Now the effect is neutralized.

Why It Matters

Because the Doc Fee is often:

👉 One of the easiest ways for dealerships to quietly increase profit

Without changing:

The advertised price
The monthly payment (noticeably)
The perceived deal

Doc Fee vs. OTD Price

This is where everything connects.

The Doc Fee is just **one component** of the:

👉 **Out-the-Door (OTD) Price**

Which means:

👉 It should never be looked at in isolation

Only as part of the total.

What You Should Do

Always ask for a full breakdown that includes:

Selling price
Taxes
Government fees
Doc Fee
Add-ons

Then focus on:

👉 The total OTD number

Key Principle

It doesn't matter where the money is labeled—
only how much you're paying in total.

Bottom Line

The Doc Fee is a standard part of most car deals...

...but it is also a built-in profit center for the dealership.

You may not eliminate it.

👉 But you can neutralize it by negotiating the total deal.

Delivery, Processing & Handling (DPH) 🚚

👉 This is **NOT the same as the doc fee**

✔ **What it is:**

Charged by **Toyota (the manufacturer)**
Covers:
Transport from factory → port → dealership
Logistics & handling
Distribution costs
🧠 **Key point:**
Every single Toyota has this fee — at every dealership

👉 You cannot:
Negotiate it away ❌
Remove it ❌

Down Payment

The amount of money paid upfront when purchasing a vehicle. It reduces the total loan amount, lowers monthly payments, and can decrease the total interest paid over the life of the loan.

Credit Score

A numerical rating (typically ranging from 300 to 850) that represents a buyer's creditworthiness. It directly impacts loan approval, interest rates, and financing terms—the higher the score, the better the loan conditions.

Monthly Payment

The amount paid each month toward a vehicle loan. It includes principal and interest, and sometimes additional costs such as taxes, fees, and add-ons. While commonly used in negotiations, focusing only on the monthly payment can hide the true total cost of the vehicle.

Bumper-to-Bumper Warranty

A type of vehicle warranty that covers most components of the car from front to back ("bumper to bumper"), excluding normal wear-and-tear items such as tires, brake pads, and maintenance-related parts. Typically limited by time or mileage (e.g., 3 years/36,000 miles).

Day Supply (Days' Supply of Inventory)

A measurement of how long a dealership's current inventory will last based on the current sales pace. For example, a 60-day supply means the dealer has enough vehicles to last 60 days without receiving new inventory. Higher day supply can increase a buyer's negotiating leverage.

Buy Rate

The lowest interest rate a lender approves for a buyer based on their credit profile. Dealers may mark up this rate when presenting financing options, keeping the difference as additional profit.

Sell Rate

The interest rate the dealership presents to the customer for financing the vehicle. It is often higher than the **buy rate** (the rate approved by the lender), with the difference kept by the dealership as additional profit. This markup is typically negotiable, though many buyers are unaware it exists.

🔥 *"The buy rate is what you qualify for. The sell rate is what they hope you accept."* 🔥

Delivery, Processing, and Handling (DPH Fee)

A fee charged by the manufacturer to cover the cost of transporting the vehicle from the factory to the dealership, as well as handling and logistics. This fee is typically non-negotiable and is included on the window sticker, though it often appears as part of the overall vehicle price.

Allocation Swap

It's a dealer trade, which allows one dealership to have a vehicle being delivered to them instead of the original dealership destination assigned at the time of manufacturing.

Below-the-Line Money

Manufacturer payments made to the dealership that are **not visible to the customer** and are not included in the invoice price. These hidden incentives increase the dealer's actual profit beyond the apparent margin.

Advertising Assistance

A manufacturer incentive paid to the dealership to help cover marketing and advertising costs for a vehicle. This payment is typically hidden from the buyer and can add additional profit to the dealer (e.g., around $400 on a $40,000 vehicle).

Floor Plan Assistance

Money paid by the manufacturer to help dealerships offset the cost of financing their inventory. Since dealers often borrow money to keep cars on the lot, this assistance reduces their carrying costs and effectively increases their profit (e.g., around $800 in some cases).

Holdback

A percentage of the vehicle's base MSRP (typically 1.5% to 3%) that the manufacturer pays back to the dealer after the vehicle is sold. This payment is usually made periodically (often quarterly) and represents additional hidden profit for the dealership.

True Dealer Cost (Real Cost)

The dealership's actual cost for a vehicle after factoring in all manufacturer incentives such as holdback, advertising assistance, and floor plan assistance. This number is often **significantly lower than the invoice price**, even though customers are rarely aware of it.

Total Dealer Profit

The full profit a dealership earns from selling a vehicle, including both visible margin (invoice to MSRP) and hidden incentives (below-the-line money). In many cases, the real profit can be **double what the customer believes it is**.

Market Adjustment (Dealer Markup)

An additional charge added by the dealership on top of MSRP due to supply and demand. It is often labeled as "Market Adjustment" or "ADM" (Additional Dealer Markup).

This fee does not reflect added value to the vehicle—it is purely additional profit based on market conditions.

👉 Example:
MSRP: $40,000
Market Adjustment: +$5,000
Selling Price: $45,000

👉 This fee is always negotiable—even when dealers say it isn't.

Add-Ons (Dealer Installed Accessories)

Optional or pre-installed products added by the dealership to increase profit. These may include:

Paint protection
Theft protection systems
Window tint
VIN etching
Tracking devices

These items are often overpriced and may already be installed before the customer sees the vehicle, creating pressure to accept them.

👉 Many add-ons can be declined or negotiated.

Extended Warranty (Vehicle Service Contract)

A paid protection plan that extends coverage beyond the manufacturer's original warranty. Despite the name, it is typically not a true "warranty," but a service contract sold for additional cost.

Often sold in the finance office and marked up significantly.

👉 Can usually be purchased later—and often for less.

GAP Insurance (Guaranteed Asset Protection)

Coverage that pays the difference between what you owe on your loan and the vehicle's actual value if it is totaled or stolen.

Example:
Loan balance: $30,000
Car value: $20,000

👉 GAP covers the $10,000 difference.

Often useful in certain situations—but frequently overpriced at dealerships.

Loan Term

The length of time you agree to repay your vehicle loan (e.g., 60 months, 72 months, 84 months).

Longer loan terms reduce monthly payments but increase the total interest paid and the overall cost of the vehicle.

👉 Lower payment does NOT mean a better deal.

Negative Equity (Upside Down Loan)

A situation where you owe more on your vehicle than it is worth.

Example:

Loan balance: $25,000
Car value: $18,000

👉 Negative equity: $7,000

This amount is often rolled into a new loan when trading in a vehicle, increasing total debt.

Pre-Approval

A financing offer from a bank or credit union obtained before visiting the dealership. It provides a baseline interest rate and loan terms.

👉 This is one of the strongest tools a buyer can bring into a negotiation.

It helps prevent interest rate markups by the dealership.

Doc Fee vs Government Fees (Clarification Term)

You already defined Doc Fee well—but adding this distinction strengthens it:
👉 Government Fees are legitimate, fixed costs (title, registration, taxes)
👉 Doc Fee is dealership-controlled and often inflated

This helps readers clearly separate **real costs vs profit padding.**

Back-End Profit

Profit made after the vehicle sale, primarily through financing, warranties, insurance products, and add-ons.

👉 Most dealership profit lives here—not in the car price.

Front-End Profit

Profit made on the vehicle itself (difference between selling price and dealer cost).

👉 Usually smaller than back-end profit.

Payment Packing

The practice of adding extra products (warranties, GAP, etc.) into the monthly payment without clearly disclosing them individually.

👉 The customer sees a payment... not the hidden items inside it.

Four-Square Method

A traditional dealership negotiation worksheet that mixes:

Price
Trade-in
Down payment
Monthly payment

☞ Designed to confuse buyers and shift numbers between categories.

Disposition Fee

A Disposition Fee is a charge applied at the end of a lease when the vehicle is returned to the leasing company instead of being purchased or replaced with another lease from the same lender.

It is intended to cover the cost of:

Inspecting the vehicle
Cleaning and reconditioning
Transporting the car to auction or resale channels

Typical Range:

☞ $300 – $500 (varies by manufacturer and lender)

Key Details:

The fee is only charged if you **return the vehicle and walk away**
It is often **waived** if you lease or purchase another vehicle from the same brand or financing company

It is disclosed in the original lease agreement but is often overlooked by buyers

Key Principle:

👉 The disposition fee is not a surprise—it's a **predefined exit cost** built into the lease.

Bottom Line:

If you plan to return the vehicle at lease-end, expect to pay a disposition fee—unless you stay within the same brand and qualify for a waiver.

ACKNOWLEDGMENTS

To my daughters:

Brianna Angelina Templar (10) — my teammate, my strategist, my best buddy.
Whether we are playing soccer, building ideas, filming, or simply thinking out loud together, you meet me with clarity, courage, and curiosity. You remind me that the best decisions in life—on the field or at the table—come from presence, awareness, and trust. You don't just share moments with me... you sharpen me. And for that, I am endlessly grateful.

Hazel Autumn Templar (8) — my artist, my heart, my reminder of what truly matters.
In a world full of numbers, negotiations, and outcomes, you bring me back to something deeper—truth without strategy, expression without calculation. Your kindness, your creativity, and your sincerity are grounding forces in my life. You remind me that not everything is meant to be won... some things are simply meant to be felt.

Mackenzie Arwen Templar (3) — my quiet partner in stillness.
In the late hours, when the world slows down and everything becomes silent, you are there. You've taught me patience, presence, and the kind of awareness that cannot be rushed. The same awareness that wins in life... long before any negotiation ever begins.

To my wife, **Gelsey Aidan Templar** — my foundation, my balance, and my reality check.
Every system I study, every strategy I refine, every word I write...

stands on the stability you create. You hold the structure so I can explore the edges. You remind me that control is not force—it is steadiness. And because of you, everything I build has ground beneath it.

To **The Monroe Institute**, and especially **Joe McMoneagle**, for opening doors that go far beyond logic, beyond strategy, and beyond what most people believe is possible. And for gifting me **three hours** of your precious time for my *Templar Truths* podcast.

To the trainers of:

- Gateway Voyage (**Charleene Nicely & Maya Grey**)
- Lifeline (**Ellen Jones-Walker & Tip Walker**)
- Spoon Bending (**Maya Grey & Luca Biotti**)
- Connecting With Your Guides (**Allyn Evans & Luigi Sciambarella**)
- Remote Viewing (**Joe McMoneagle & Beth Vaughan & Deryn Winchester**)

Thank you for teaching me that true awareness is the ultimate advantage—whether in consciousness... or across a negotiation table.

To **Alyssa Citarella**,
for your guidance, your patience, and your generosity of spirit. Thank you for welcoming me into the **Dolphin Energy Club (DEC)** and for answering my millions of questions with clarity, kindness, and depth. You made the unfamiliar feel understood... and the complex feel simple.

And finally...

To the unseen dynamics that govern both life and negotiation:

To timing.
To silence.
To awareness.
To the moment before a decision is made.

Because every deal...
every outcome...
every path...

is shaped long before words are spoken.

This book is not just about buying a car.

It is about seeing clearly.
Thinking independently.
And standing your ground in a world designed to move you.

With loyalty, clarity, and control,
Benjamin A. Templar
Knight of the Dealerships Rebels ⚔️🚘

ABOUT THE AUTHOR

Benjamin A. Templar is a writer, award-winning actor, filmmaker, and certified *Master Life Coaching Professional.* His work bridges storytelling, healing, and transformation, with a voice rooted in lived experience, creative passion, and a deep respect for personal growth.

In 2012, he studied at the William Esper Studio in New York City, where he trained under respected mentors and refined his craft with discipline and passion. That training laid the groundwork for a career marked by emotional depth and creative risk.

Templar's presence on screen has been defined by his compelling performances and deep commitment to storytelling. His portrayal of Manny DiStefano in the cult-favorite post-apocalyptic series *Plaga Zombie* solidified his status as a dynamic actor with a memorable on-screen presence. Over the years, his versatility has been showcased in more than 30 independent films, where he has played roles ranging from soulful leads to gritty antiheroes.

His talent has earned him two Best Actor awards—one from The Actors Awards Film Festival and another from the Festigious International Film Festival—for his performance in *The Street Photographer*, a film he also directed. Whether on set or on screen, Templar brings authenticity, intensity, and a clear devotion to the art of film.

In 2021, he founded SunBow Media LLC and expanded into filmmaking, directing *The Street Photographer*, which went on to win Best Sci-Fi Film at the Buenos Aires Indie Film Awards. His presence —both behind and in front of the camera—is always fueled by a desire to tell stories that matter.

Ben is also the author of several books, including *Masterplan Your Success*, *We Are The Aliens*, *Goodbye Toxic People*, and *Princely Chess*, a creative reimagining of classic chess. His latest book, *Unsubscribe Them: The Subtle Act of Not Giving a Sub*, is a manifesto on emotional boundaries and personal sovereignty, examining how disengaging from toxic relationships, digital noise, and false obligations can restore clarity and peace.

He is also an **AI music designer** *(also known as a music producer)* and the creator of a new music genre called ***Templar Chants****—a fusion of Gregorian chants and cinematic music scores.*

He holds a degree in *Computer Systems Management* (A.S.) from the Community College of Vermont, graduating *Magna Cum Laude* and inducted into the *Phi Theta Kappa Honor Society*. Before dedicating himself fully to the arts and coaching, he worked in healthcare and digital mapping, supporting people and systems with quiet precision.

Above all, Ben is a husband, a father to three daughters, and a man who believes that loyalty, love, and legacy matter. Inspired by the values of the Knights Templar, his life and work reflect a commitment to courage, clarity, and spiritual purpose.

facebook.com/BenjaminTemplar
instagram.com/benjamintemplar
x.com/BenjaminTemplar
linkedin.com/in/benjamintemplar

ALSO BY BENJAMIN A. TEMPLAR

EarthQuakers: A Religious Constitutional Manual and Ethical Spiritual Guide

Pures LeBen Soul Advancement Center: The Soul Exchange Marketplace?

Unsubscribe Them: The Subtle Act of Not Giving a Sub

Quote by Quote: A Curated Chronological Anthology of Life-Transforming Quotes

SIBO Yogurt Mastery: The Most Efficient Gallon-a-Week Workflow

Princely Chess: What Happens When the Prince Joins the Battle? Master Chess's Secret Heir with Easy Rules and Endless Fun

Goodbye Toxic People: Forgive Them But Forget Them Forever: How to Cleanse These Toxins from Your Life

We Are The Aliens: Saving Earth from Alien AI Conquest

TransNationals: Reclaiming Your National Identity Beyond Birth

Divine Incomparable You (D. I. Y.): How to Rebuild Your Soul's Temple: From Childhood Soul Splitting Trauma to Soul Remerging and Becoming the 2.0 Version of Yourself

Masterplan Your Success: Deadline Your Dreams

How to Buy a Car at the Dealership: And Not Get Ripped Off That Badly

Templar Library of Public Domain Classics (Editor)

Dollars Want Me: A Timeless Guide to Attracting Wealth and Financial Abundance

(by Henry Harrison Brown, edited and modernized by Benjamin A. Templar)

Made in the USA
Monee, IL
13 September 2026

62981863R00193